Creative
Ecumenical
Education

Creative Ecumenical Education

Learning from One Another

Simon Oxley

WCC Publications, Geneva

Cover design: Rob Lucas
Cover illustration: WCC Photo Library

ISBN 2-8254-1363-1

© 2002, WCC Publications, World Council of Churches
150 route de Ferney, P.O. Box 2100
1211 Geneva 2, Switzerland
Web site: http://www.wcc-coe.org

No. 98 in the Risk Book Series

Printed in Switzerland

Contents

vii   PREFACE

1   INTRODUCTION: MAP-READERS OR MAP-MAKERS

7   1. EDUCATION OR FORMATION: DOES
    WHAT IT'S CALLED MATTER?

23   2. ECUMENICAL EDUCATION: IN PRACTICE

37   3. BREAKING THE BOUNDARIES OF THINKING

53   4. LEARNING AS THE ESSENCE OF FAITH

70   5. HOW WE LEARN TOGETHER

93   6. TEACHING, RESOURCES AND LEARNING

114   7. SPECTATORS OR PARTICIPANTS?

127   8. REARRANGING THE CHAIRS
    AND OURSELVES

140   CONCLUSION MOVING ON

147   SUGGESTIONS FOR FURTHER READING

Preface

When I joined the staff of the World Council of Churches (WCC) in 1996, I soon wondered what I was doing here. Having spent my whole working life and much of my spare time involved with different forms of education, I understood education as a total and lifelong process. Although there were several education-related desks spread across the organization, we seemed to have no collective and integrated understanding and practice of education in the ecumenical movement.

I found a purpose for being here when I became involved in developing and implementing a staff team on Education and Ecumenical Formation as part of the reorganization of the WCC following the 1998 Harare assembly. Our discussions around ecumenical learning as the prime focus of the new team gave me a renewed sense of purpose for our work.

I want to acknowledge that without my colleagues in the Education and Ecumenical Formation team, this book would not have been possible. I have borrowed their best ideas and they have stimulated my thinking. In the same way, other WCC colleagues and participants in consultations, workshops and conferences have helped me develop my thinking and my practice. This book is neither a summary of their experiences nor even my final word on ecumenical education, but a contribution to the continuous process of learning in which we must all be involved if we are to be true to our ecumenical calling.

There are many people to whom I am grateful, but they will have to forgive me if I only name three. Jan Kok, who, sadly, died in February 2002, encouraged me to write this. Even as a fellow supporter of Servette Football Club, Geneva, his responsibilities to WCC Publications meant that it had to be a book on education rather than football! Two friends, Beth Godfrey and Christy Lohr, generously gave their own time, when they could have been doing something more interesting, to variously suggest ideas, share their knowledge, demand progress reports and read what I had written.

For you, the reader, what I hope is that, one way or another, I will have given you some impetus to make your education both ecumenical and creative.

Simon Oxley
Geneva, 2002

Introduction

Map-readers or Map-makers?

> "Education must, as it were, simultaneously provide maps of a complex world in constant turmoil and the compass that will enable people to find their way within it."
>
> – *Learning: The Treasure Within*, International Commission on Education for the Twenty-first Century, UNESCO, 1996.
>
> Think of your own experience of education in the church setting and in school or college. Does this quotation describe your experience? If not, can you think of an image that would better describe it?
>
> What do you see as the strengths and weaknesses of this description of education?

As you can see, you are expected to do some work as you read this book! It was difficult for me to conceive of writing this book without involving the reader in the process of learning. Indeed, it would be illogical to use the monologue of writing to advocate an ecumenical education that is essentially participative and interactive.

At the start of every chapter and elsewhere you will find some questions or exercises. These are designed to help you bring your experience and knowledge to the reading of this book so that it can become a more effective learning exercise. What I write is not the "right answer" against which you can judge the correctness of your own responses. Rather, it is a contribution to the discussion we must have if we are to learn what creative ecumenical education can be in our own context.

If I confess that much of my early success in mathematics at school was because the textbooks had the answers in the back, you will begin to understand my early experience of education. The emphasis was on getting the right answer using a given formula, without much concern for the underlying principles on which the answer was based. This meant that, when confronted with a different kind of mathematical problem that could not be solved by one of these procedures, there was no means of working out a solution from underlying principles.

The same was true of other subject areas. There were certain facts to memorize and repeat on appropriate occasions such as in examinations. The facts gained their truth not because I understood them, but because the teacher or the textbook said so. To give one example, it is very instructive for English people to visit the exhibition of the Bayeaux Tapestry in the town of that name in France. As an English schoolchild, I learned that the Battle of Hastings in 1066 was a story of a brave English king, Harold, attempting to resist an invasion by the Norman French duke, William. Visitors to the tapestry exhibition, however, see a different version of events: William had the right to become king of England and had Harold's support. But Harold saw an opportunity to take power for himself and reneged on the agreement. This prompted an armed invasion rather than a natural succession. It is much easier, but ultimately misleading, to see history as a set of facts rather than judgments and interpretations.

In Sunday school, I had the same experience. I learned many things about Jesus and my faith development was framed by "I believe that ... " rather than "I relate to or I believe in ..." There were right answers about many things that did not relate to my experience of life, but little help in making sense of my life and the world in which I lived from the basis of Christian faith. Later in life, as an ecumenical university chaplain, I saw the results when deeply committed believers schooled in learning the "facts" of faith were confronted with questions to which they had no readily prepared right answers. Their home churches probably blamed this confusion on the fact that their students were let loose in a dangerous world of ideas when the real failure may have been in not equipping them to think and believe for themselves.

Travel directions

In the light of all this, it will come as no surprise that I did not recognize the image of the map and compass in my own early educational experiences. The image I would use is that of the travel directions someone might give to help you travel from one place to another. Where to turn left or right is clearly indicated with reference to the signposts or prominent features of the townscape or countryside. There is only one course indicated and no help to find the way if, by need or chance, you make a detour. The usefulness of such travel directions depends on how well what is written corresponds with the reality on the ground. As many of us find to our cost on our journeys, things change — the wording on signposts is altered and buildings are redeveloped and unrecognizable. Unless constantly updated, such travel directions do not serve the traveller well. As useful as they are, there is no universal and constantly relevant set of travel directions for everyday journeys or for life.

There is much to be said for the map and compass as an image for education. It recognizes that we need to be equipped to find our way through a world that is constantly increasing in complexity. The sport of orienteering is based on the competitors' ability to read a map to get them from checkpoint to checkpoint as much as on their athleticism in running over difficult terrain. Those who read the map the wrong way up will run off in the wrong direction. A compass is necessary to orient the map correctly. Education should give us more than one tool to help us make our journey at our own speed. We can only rewrite the travel directions given yesterday by religion, science or any other discipline if we are prepared to find the way using the maps and compass available to us.

There is a continuing debate in churches and in educational institutions between those who believe that education is all about giving people travel directions and those who believe that it is about giving them a map and compass so that they can find their way. It can be caricatured as "traditionalist" against "progressive" in educational and theological terms. However, both could claim to be drawing on Christian truth and there are many ways in which the Bible, Christian doctrine and Jesus himself can be enlisted to support either position. In theological terms, this is not a debate between "conservatives" and "liberals". Both can be highly directive in the way we should go; equally, both can be open to a more explorative approach to education.

Much has been written in the political sphere about a "third way" that straddles or negates the socialist/capitalist divide. I want to propose a third image to add to those of travel directions and the map and compass. This is not an integrating image but one that many will find very uncomfortable. I am indebted to what may seem an unlikely source for stimulating this thought. In his book *The Road Ahead*, Bill Gates, the founder of computer giant Microsoft, observes that there is never a reliable map for unexplored territory and that the journey of discovery into unknown territory is exciting. Developments in information technology and genetic engineering or an understanding of how globalization works are examples of unexplored territory for humanity. It is not a matter of being unsure which way up to hold the map, but the difficulty that no map may yet exist. At a more personal level, changed patterns of living and behaving in many societies are as yet unmapped.

Map-makers

The third image I propose is learning to be explorers and map-makers. To continue the analogy, our tools are even more basic than a map and compass; they are blank sheets of paper, coloured pens, a sense of adventure and an enquiring mind. This image may seem a long way away from people's experiences of church or school. Perhaps this is more a criticism of lifeless institutions than of the image.

Why should anyone want to go to the trouble of being a map-maker when there are more than enough maps and travel guides on the bookshop shelves? A danger of using images, analogies or metaphors is that the concrete actuality may limit the concept it helps illustrate. Our travel is through life and not only through a landscape. Life, which in our context must be understood to include faith, has elements of global commonality from our humanity and local commonality in our societal and religious communities. To a certain extent, therefore, there is a common "landscape" to be mapped. Yet my life is not the same as yours, even though we may have much in common. The same is true of communities, for in ecumenical education we are dealing with the collective as well as the individual. This requires us as individuals and communities to draw our own map of the territory we occupy or through which we travel.

In giving this book the title *Creative Ecumenical Education,* I was conscious of using "creative" in two ways. My first reason was to describe productive and innovative ways of engaging people in learning. So I hope this book will encourage creativity in reflecting on, planning and doing ecumenical education. My basic reason, however, was that I believe that ecumenical education should be about creating — creating understanding, openness, commitment, engagement and action.

Rather than only helping adults and children become better direction followers or map-readers, we should be encouraging them to be map-makers, a more exciting and creative process.

1. Education or Formation: Does What It's Called Matter?

> Think of the two words "education" and "formation". How would you define each of them?
>
> What difference does it make when we add the word "ecumenical" to either of them?
>
> Don't look in a dictionary or anywhere else; use only your own knowledge and experience.

There are probably not many similarities between the eastern side of London and the Holy Land. One is that there are Christians, Jews and Muslims living alongside one another. The basic objective of the Encounter project is facilitating dialogue and encounter between young people of those faiths from England and the Holy Land. While recognizing and respecting the differences between Christians, Jews and Muslims, it aims to enable young people to explore common values and visions.

The project is a church initiative but also involves mosques and synagogues in both places. It is also an example of what I mean by creative ecumenical education.

One of the differences among us in the ecumenical movement is our definition of what it means to be young! In the Encounter project young people were defined as those between the ages of 16 and 19. Twelve young people were chosen from each place, four from each faith, with an equal number of males and females. They were accompanied in their experiences by adults drawn from both regions and from each faith. In 1999 they spent two weeks together in the Holy Land and in 2000 they spent two weeks in London. The group of young people was virtually identical for both visits, allowing relationships between them to develop. They visited each other's places of worship and had opportunities for discussion with religious leaders. They were involved in workshops and seminars and enjoyed leisure activities together.

The possibilities for interaction in this project are enormous. Most obviously there is the encounter between people of different faiths and the encounter between those who live in England and those who live in the Holy Land. But there is a greater richness than this. Being a Christian in London is not the same as being a Palestinian Christian. Being a Jew in London is not the same as being a Jew in Israel. Being a Palestinian Muslim is not the same as being a Muslim in England with family roots in Pakistan.

Of equal, if not greater, significance is that the young people from England may not have engaged with one another across their different faiths without this project. The same is true for the young people from the Holy Land. I wonder if it was easier for engagement to occur in the more neutral space of this project where the young people were either the host community or guests. Finding yourself in the same category, host or guest, may help open you to encounter whereas being categorized according to faith may be too strong for genuine encounter.

When asked whether the two-year project had changed them in any way, the young people answered:

"I've learned to listen to, respect and understand other people's viewpoints and opinions, to accept other people's feelings and needs."

"I learned not to judge people from outside and to listen to and respect others."

It can never be too early in your life to learn such things, but it can be too late.

From the experience of the Encounter project we can extract a number of important characteristics of creative ecumenical education. Namely, ecumenical education:

- begins with people's actual context – religious, social, political – and builds on the experience and knowledge they bring;
- is not only about sharing each other's knowledge, but discovering new knowledge; encounter opens us up to the "other" to learn from and with them – the other person, the other way of believing, acting or thinking;
- breaks through the barriers we build between us – of race, gender, sexual orientation, culture, religion, class, poli-

tics, economics, etc. – and enables our differences to become a resource for learning;
- builds community towards the unity of the church, of humanity and of creation;
- is people learning together in community;
- means communities as well as individuals learning;
- is open and participatory;
- involves reflection and action;
- is a holistic process that unites the physical, social and spiritual;
- is not so much learning about the ecumenical movement as becoming ecumenical in attitude and practice.

Creative ecumenical education is how we turn these desires into reality!

We can find ecumenical education happening in formal education (in universities, seminaries, laity centres and schools), in congregations (in Sunday schools, Bible study groups and discussion groups), through church-related networks and organizations focusing on particular issues (in development education and campaigns), and through the business of everyday life.

Education or formation

We were sitting, shaded from the hot Cuban sun, discussing ecumenical theological education in Latin America. "We should not use the word education but instead talk of formation," one of the participants said to the group. He went on to explain that in his context, education had negative connotations and was something to be resisted. It was all about controlling people and their learning. Education happened so that the state or the church could produce the kind of people it needed. In the case of the state, it needed people who would be able to contribute to the economy and be compliant citizens. In the case of the church, it needed people who would accept its worship, doctrine and discipline. Formation, on the other hand, was a process that opened people up to life and liberated them. The learning objectives of formation were not imposed by institutions for their own purposes but developed by learners in their context.

As I listened, I totally agreed with his analysis except from one thing. I would have used the words in exactly the opposite manner. In its essence, education should be liberative and open-ended. For me, however, formation implies that we know the "end product" of the process – a kind of person, a particular set of skills, a special kind of knowledge. Formation works only to produce a desired result.

This problem of terminology partly arises from a varying use of the words in different contexts. The ecumenical movement is also a multilingual environment and there is never a one-to-one correspondence between words in different languages. Some readers may have reacted without enthusiasm to the title of this book because it contains the word education. For others, it may be the reason they picked it up.

Having noted this problem, we will concentrate on reflecting on what we mean by ecumenical education or ecumenical formation in practice. For the sake of consistency, I will use the term education instead of formation, rather than alternating or always using both terms.

We will begin thinking about ecumenical education by briefly placing it in the context of the development of the modern ecumenical movement and, particularly, the work of the WCC. In the 19th century, laypeople met together, often to the annoyance of their churches, to support the work of Christian education, usually in the form of Sunday schools. Interchurch groups prepared teaching resources for use by local congregations and Sunday schools. National associations were formed in many countries and in 1889 the first World Sunday School Convention was held. The resulting global organization became the World Council for Christian Education, which merged with the WCC in 1971. If this was not ecumenical education, it was the beginning of ecumenical collaboration in education.

From the early part of the 20th century, the practice and outcomes of ecumenism have been studied. Following the Evanston assembly of the World Council in 1954, the newly created Division of Ecumenical Action reflected on ecumenical education and reported to the 1957 meeting of the central committee:

> Ecumenical education can no longer be limited to the history of attempts to reunite churches or the growth of ecumenical organizations. Ecumenical education essentially means fostering understanding of, commitment to and informed participation in, this whole ecumenical process.

We might be surprised that, at this early stage, while enthusiasm for the ecumenical movement was still running high, a tradition had begun of ecumenical education as a study of the past rather than as inspiring and equipping people to participate in an ongoing and future-directed process. Forty-five years later, we may wonder whether the practice of ecumenical education has yet fully changed from studying the ecumenical movement to becoming ecumenical in practice.

Participation in ecumenical education was again emphasized at the 1975 WCC assembly in Nairobi. However, we see a development in the understanding of the term ecumenical. The assumption in 1957 was that ecumenical education was basically about the unity of the church. Now ecumenical education is about the human community in interaction with the community of the church.

> ... Programmes should challenge the churches beyond the brokenness of our human situation as well as beyond the partial, incomplete character of our ecumenical effort towards deeper sustained and sustaining relationships. If this is to happen, all member churches must be helped to participate in the process of ecumenical education that is so fundamental to our pilgrimage.[1]

In addition to a development of understanding of education, there also has been an expansion of the domain of ecumenism. Taking the root meaning of the word *oikoumene* in the Greek of the gospels as the whole inhabited earth, ecumenical education developed a concern for all that made for fullness of life for humanity. The dynamic unity of the church was integrally connected with broader issues of justice and peace. The context of humanity – the global environment – also became important for the ecumenical movement.

The roots through which the ecumenical movement draws its life and purpose are in the churches. The WCC remains no more and no less than a global fellowship of churches. In recent years, however, we have seen the further extension by some of ecumenism beyond the Christian faith to a movement of world faiths. This is not to be confused with the work of dialogue with the other world faiths that for many years has been an important aspect of the ecumenical movement. Some metropolitan ecumenical bodies in the United States, for example, are interfaith organizations.

Ecumenical learning

Part of the learning we do together must be to understand what ecumenical might be in our local context and at the global level. Philip Potter, giving his general secretary's report to the Vancouver assembly of the WCC in 1983, emphasized the churches as a community of learning. Through relating to God we should be opened up to a wider vision and to common action. In the 1980s, the WCC twice brought people together from around the world to reflect on the understanding and practice of what was by then known as ecumenical learning. The fruits of this are seen in the publication in 1989 of the WCC resource *Alive Together – a Practical Guide to Ecumenical Learning*. The book offers three definitions of ecumenical learning:

> 1. Learning which enables people, while remaining rooted in one tradition of the church, to become open and responsive to the richness and perspectives of other churches, so that they become more active in seeking unity, openness and collaboration between churches.
>
> Learning which enables people of one country, language, ethnic group, class or political and economic system, to become sensitive and responsive to those of other countries, ethnic groups, political and economic situations, so that they become active participants in action for a more just world.

2. Ecumenical learning is what happens when diverse persons, rooted in their own faith traditions and complex experiences of culture, gender, nationality, race, call, etc., become open and responsive to the richness of perspectives in the struggle of others, together seeking to know God and to be faithful to God's intention for them in their world.

3. Ecumenical learning is a process by which:
– diverse groups and individuals;
– well rooted in their own faith, traditions, cultures and contexts;
– are enabled to risk honest encounters with one another before God;
– as they study and struggle together in community;
– with personally relevant issues;
– in the light of the scriptures, the traditions of their faith, worship and global realities;
– resulting in communal action in faithfulness to God's intention for the unity of the church and humankind, and for justice, peace and the integrity of creation.[2]

It seems that the recommendation to the WCC central committee in 1957 that ecumenical education should encourage and enable participation had really had an effect. There is no trace in the 1989 resource of an ecumenical education that examines the past. The only concern of ecumenical learning, as it is described, is the present reality. If there is any engagement with the past it is with the traditions of the churches, not of the ecumenical movement. Does this position reflect today's reality?

From my observation, the tendency for ecumenical education to concentrate on the history of the work to bring unity to the churches and of the activity of ecumenical organizations is alive and well. If there is a weakness in what we do, it is still in enabling participation. It is important that we know the ecumenical journey we have taken to come to this point in time. We do need to be able to access all that has been learned in the ecumenical movement through success and failure along the way. We are already familiar with this general principle, otherwise we would have given up on reading the Bible! (In reading the Bible, we encounter writings that interpret the past in their own contexts at the same time we interpret those historical writings in our own context. Both help us understand and draw from the journey taken so far.)

"Reception" and "ecumenical memory" are two terms frequently used within the ecumenical movement. The need for these is often stressed. Reception refers to a process by which the outcomes of a study process or a conference are taken into the thinking and activity of the churches and related networks. Ecumenical memory is the knowledge of what has already been done within the ecumenical movement in terms of issues considered and actions taken. However, both terms can be problematic for ecumenical education.

Reception can so easily be taken to imply a process whereby some do the thinking and the rest should receive the results of their work and put it into practice. I hear complaints that this or that piece of good work was done ecumenically but the churches took no notice of it. Sometimes there is an implicit criticism that if the educators had done their job more effectively, everyone would be aware and engaged. It is easy to identify some of the problems with this in terms of both attitude and process. It betrays an "us-and-them" attitude. It clearly separates those who discern, reflect and strategize from those who are to act, and sets the ecumenical movement apart as something parallel to and separate from the churches. It also indicates a process that has not directly involved anyone else apart from the participants in the particular study or conference. Asking the question about reception once the work has been done, or presuming from the beginning that all we need to say is "now get on with it" are sure signs of a fatally flawed process.

In addressing the fifth world conference on Faith and Order, Catholicos Aram I, currently moderator of the WCC central committee, reflected on the bilateral theological dialogues that have taken place between churches. He called for a process of reception that was not simply about the formal adoption of statements but included "effective communication, dynamic interpretation and ecumenical conscientization. This process of reception implies ecumenical education and conversion and mutual accountability."[3] The role of ecumenical education is not to sell ecumenical thought or action to the churches at the national or congregational level. Rather it is engaging with people and opening up attitudes and processes.

The importance of knowing where the ecumenical journey has taken us so far and the need to use that knowledge to draw our contemporary maps is self-evident. However, ecumenical memory also has the potential to inhibit ecumenical learning. It may be used overtly to control the agenda of ecumenical education by determining what does or does not need to be learned. In a subtler way, it may predispose us to a limited understanding of the boundaries and possibilities of ecumenical education. To make a comparison, none of the great moments of scientific discovery would have been possible if the process of learning had been entirely under the control of "scientific memory".

Sometimes people who have been involved in a learning exercise can be critical of those who repeat it and come up with similar outcomes – why didn't they just read our report? Real ecumenical education, however, will sometimes demand that people do it for themselves. I cannot simply take someone else's travel book off the shelf and read it as a substitute for making my own journey. We do not need to be proprietary and defensive about what we have learned; instead, we should use our experience to encourage others to actively learn, too, even if it appears to be a duplication of effort.

One of the skills that ecumenical education needs to teach is that of critical discernment. Then we can carry with us from the past what we need for today. What has been discovered, said, done or learned ecumenically may be interesting information. The many shelves occupied by reports produced by the World Council and other ecumenical councils and agencies should remind us of the weight of experience, knowledge and understanding that has been amassed by the ecumenical movement. The time for some of the thinking has now gone. Honesty might compel us to admit that, for some of the work, the time never was. Perhaps there are things for which the time is still to come. For people who are called to travel light, it is a mighty burden to drag along. There is also ecumenical memory, which is light – that is, the ecumenical memory that is carried in the living faith and activity of communities and people.

Something needs to happen to make our ecumenical past contribute to our present ecumenical experience and activity. This is not something strange to Christians. Sunday by Sunday, in a variety of ways, the command of Jesus to "do this in memory of me" is obeyed. In bread and wine the past is brought into the present in a living tradition. Through ecumenical education we can learn how to use ecumenical memory, not just how to store it.

Transformation versus transmission

It may also help us to think about education itself. All too often we think of education only as what happens in school, college or university. The late Brazilian educator Paulo Freire questioned conventional thinking and practice in the types of education used in schooling. In his writing and in his own educational activities he challenged a "banking" concept of education. In the banking model, the teacher (who is knowledgeable) pays in information that is saved up by the individual learner (who initially knows nothing). A teacher conveys selected, pre-packaged information to passive learners. Freire believed that education should be liberating, that it should be about the action of knowing or understanding rather than the transfer of information. Control of the process of learning does not rest with the teacher but is a shared responsibility through which teachers and learners all grow through a process of dialogue. Learning begins with the themes at the heart of peoples' own experience – their concepts, values, hopes and fears-rather than being required by an externally imposed curriculum. For Freire, education is always a collective experience. It is a process of empowerment for the community as well as the individual.

There are two significant words associated with Freire's educational work that emphasize the distance from conventional schooling: "conscientization" (in Portuguese, *conscientização*) and "praxis". Put simply, conscientization is a process by which people discover and understand for themselves the social and cultural realities that shape their lives, and develop their ability to change them. Praxis is a learning cycle that lies at the heart of conscientization. It is a process in which action is followed by reflection. From the reflection on the action, a new action emerges and the process repeats itself. My personal conviction is that ecumenical education should not just note this as a useful approach but use it as foundational principle.

Because of the influence of Freire and other educational thinkers, a distinction is now often drawn between transmission and transformation as the objective of education. Transmission, which we can compare to the banking concept, implies that knowledge comes from external sources and authority figures. The principal skills required by learners are those of listening, reading, observing and memorizing. Personal ideas, emotions, contributions or questions are not welcome or important. The roles of the teacher and the learner are clearly defined as giver and receiver, as the one who knows and the one who does not.

In education as transformation, learning is motivated and directed by the learner. Aesthetic, moral, emotional, physical and spiritual needs stand alongside the information and ideas. Knowledge is created and developed through a dynamic interaction among teachers, learners and multiple resources of all kinds. Teaching and learning functions become interchangeable. Unlike education as transmission, where the learners acquire a greater quantity of information, education as transformation results in a qualitative change in the learners and their contexts.

We can draw a distinction between education as transmission and as transformation, but we should not assume that the aim of handing on knowledge implicit in transmission cannot be effected by transformational education. Educational traditionalists argue that abandoning schooling models of education means that such transmission will not happen. Young people, they fear, will grow up without a knowledge of what has been experienced and learned by previous generations. Particularly sensitive areas are those of national identity and history, values and religious faith. Transformational education does not begin with a blank sheet of paper. One of the givens is that there is existing knowledge. Learners have to engage with that. However, they do not just receive it uncritically. That is the real problem for traditionalists.

By its nature, any education related to the Christian faith has to be transformational. The gospel is about change and the kingdom comes by "turning the world upside down" (Acts 17:6). Ecumenical education, in particular, is aimed at transforming individuals, communities and the world in which they live. Ecumenical education can never be content with simply handing on an ecumenical history.

Four pillars of education

Coming from a more institutional direction, the International Commission on Education for the Twenty-first Century, established by UNESCO, produced a report in 1996 called *Learning: The Treasure Within*, which identified four pillars of education-learning to know, learning to do, learning to live together and learning to be. The four are inter-related and of equal importance. Learning through education is recognized as a lifelong and life-related process that is not confined to any stage of life or institutional system. Formal and informal education are not in opposition to one another and should cross-fertilize each other.

Learning *to know* is not so much about acquiring itemized, codified information as it is about mastering the instruments of knowledge. It is no longer possible to know all there is to know, even within a limited field of knowledge. Education should stimulate intellectual curiosity. It should assist the learner to have an awareness of a broad background and to study in depth. Learning to learn is as important as acquiring particular items of knowledge.

Learning *to do* has always been an important activity, whether through formal training in industrialized economies or the informal learning of traditional skills in communities where formal employment is not the norm. The pace of global change is such that it is now difficult to envisage any such skills training that will remain relevant for the whole of a person's life. The UNESCO report identifies the need for what are sometimes called life skills (communication, teamwork, problem solving, conflict management) in addition to manual and intellectual skills.

Learning *to live together* has not always been so clearly identified as one of the basic pillars of education. Perhaps we assumed (wrongly, as experience indicates) that such learning would happen naturally or that, if we brought people into contact with one another, tolerance and respect would automatically follow. The report advocates two complementary approaches – discovering others and working towards common objectives. It suggests that to understand others, one must first know oneself. I wonder whether this is, in fact, a sequential process. It seems equally true that trying to understand others helps one know oneself.

Learning *to be* implies that education should play a role in the all around development of each individual. The report mentions intelligence, sensitivity, aesthetic sense, personal responsibility and spiritual values. Each one of us should be enabled to develop independent, critical thinking and to form our own judgment. In this way we will be able to determine for ourselves what we believe it right to do in any circumstance. While agreeing with that thinking, I believe that it needs to be qualified in a way that is not done adequately in the UNESCO report. There must be a dynamic relationship between the learning to be of the individual and the learning to be of the community of which they are a part. Each should enable the other. All the way through, the report places a strong emphasis on education in relation to the learning done by individuals. It does not similarly recognize education as a means by which communities learn, that is as entities rather than as a collection of individuals. Unless we ask some searching questions about how the four pillars of education apply to community, then our hopes for their application to individuals are likely to remain unfulfilled.

On the whole, churches have related more closely to the first two of the pillars of education. For some parts of the church, learning *to know* in the sense of acquiring information and concepts relating to Christian faith has been the prime objective of educational activity. It is as if entry to the kingdom of God is gained by passing an examination in Christianity! Some have placed an emphasis on education in church as learning how *to do* worship, prayer, pastoral care and service.

Learning *to know* and learning *to do* are important aspects of any church-related educational activity, including ecumenical education. For Christians, however, learning *to live together* and learning *to be* ought to have a special quality, for they take us close to the heart of the gospel. I say ought to because, in practice, they do not seem to be given that significance. Let us take learning to live together as an example. We can see learning to live together taken seriously, for instance, in the valuable work done by the churches through the WCC, for example, in the Programme to Combat Racism, the Justice, Peace and Integrity of Creation process, interfaith dialogue and family life education. Most recently, the churches have called each other to participate in a Decade to Overcome Violence – a wide-ranging and dedicated focus on communities and individuals living together in peace. However, such activities often seem to be regarded as additional activities for those who have that particular interest, but otherwise are just items for report on the agenda.

We know that, from the local to the global, there are groups and individuals who devote time and imagination to the whole business of learning to live together. For some there is no option because their community context demands it. Those of us for whom developing positive, sympathetic relationships with peoples from different cultures and faiths was not a life-and-death issue will have to reconsider our attitudes after the attacks on the World Trade Center and Pentagon in the United States in September 2001. If learning together and learning to be have a vital ecumenical significance, how do we ensure that they are part of the basic curriculum of churches' educational activity rather than optional extras?

The UNESCO report envisages education as being able to bring change "from narrow nationalism to universalism, from ethnic and cultural prejudice to tolerance, understanding and pluralism, from autocracy to democracy in its various manifestations and from a technologically divided world where high technology is the privilege of the few to a technologically united world"[4] Teachers are an essential catalyst in the learning process. But they have to change their role from being a soloist to an accompanist. Their task is not to hand out information and to mould learners. Rather they should help learners know how to find, organize and manage knowledge. All stakeholders in education need to be part of decision making and every learning opportunity should be democratic in structure.

As you will see, my understanding of ecumenical education is entirely sympathetic to these views put forward by the UNESCO report. Ecumenical education does not exist in its own universe. It has its own particularity but is able to draw on the experience and understanding of other forms of education and to act in partnership with them.

Think back to the answers you gave to the questions at the start of the chapter. Now read these two definitions. How well do they reflect what you might want to now say about ecumenical education?

Ecumenical formation is an ongoing process of learning within the various local churches and world communions, aimed at informing and guiding people in the movement which – inspired by the Holy Spirit – seeks the visible unity of Christians.

This pilgrimage towards unity enables mutual sharing and mutual critique through which we grow. Such an approach to unity thus involves at once rootedness in

Christ and in one's tradition, while endeavouring to discover and participate in the richness of other Christian and human traditions.

Such a response to the ecumenical imperative demands patient, humble and persistent exploration, together with people of other traditions, of the pain of our situation of separation, taking us to both the depths of our divisions and the heights of our already existing unity in the Triune God, and of the unity we hope to attain. Thus ecumenical formation is also a process of education by which we seek to orient ourselves towards God, all Christians and indeed all human beings in a spirit of renewed faithfulness to our Christian mission.

– Ecumenical Formation: Ecumenical reflections and suggestions, a study document of the Joint Working Group between the Roman Catholic Church and the World Council of Churches, May 1993

Ecumenical learning in short is the process of mutual learning from other faith and cultural traditions in the world-wide body of Christ. In intercultural exchange, dialogue, shared life and mutual encounters we experience a widening of our own limited horizons and get new impulses for living the gospel in a changing and multi-faceted world.

– Evangelical Lutheran Mission in Lower Saxony, Germany
http://bs.cyty.com/elmbs/oeku_en.htm

NOTES

[1] D.M. Paton, *Breaking Barriers: Official Report of the Fifth Assembly of the World Council of Churches*, London, SPCK, 1975, p.297.
[2] Geneva, WCC, 1989, pp. 7f.
[3] Aram I, *In Search of Ecumenical Vision*, Armenian Catholicosate of Cicilia, Antelias, 2001, pp. 95f.
[4] Jacques Delors et al., *Learning: The Treasure Within*, Paris, Unesco, 1996, pp. 141f.

2. Ecumenical Education in Practice

Have you been involved in or observed any learning process that you could describe as ecumenical education? If so, what elements of it made you want to call it ecumenical?

This chapter offers some examples of what I would describe as ecumenical education. I have not chosen them because they are perfect examples but because each contains, potentially or in practice, some of the elements most vital to ecumenical education. I hope by giving some examples of ecumenical education it will help you come to a better understanding of what it might mean in your own context. I also hope that you will resist the temptation to take one example that most appeals to you and say, "That's what ecumenical education is."

To reinforce the point, there can be no one single example of the right way of doing ecumenical education. Much will always depend on the realities of context and opportunity. If your reaction on reading these examples is that they are very interesting but hardly relevant to you, I would encourage you to learn from them what are the essential elements of ecumenical education. Then we can consider how these aspects could be applied in your situation.

Courses in Lay Leadership Training

Courses in Lay Leadership Training, often referred to as CLLTs, have offered a demanding but powerful means of ecumenical education for the past thirty years. The participants have mainly been drawn from those working with adults through laity centres. CLLTs have been organized by regional associations of laity centres, such as those for Africa or Asia. Every few years a global CLLT has been offered by OIKOSNET, the global network of laity centres, academies and movements of social concern.

The basic format of a CLLT is that of a four-week programme consisting of one week of exposure followed by three weeks of reflection and interaction. The participants are divided into groups, each of which spends one week with a different host community. All the participants then come together at one centre. Participants spend the second week sharing and reflecting on their experiences both from their own background and the exposure visits. The third week is an opportunity to work on the particular theme of the CLLT using a variety of methods. Finally, in the fourth week, participants work on how they can apply what they have learned in their own context.

To give some flesh to this, we can take the example of a CLLT held in Latin America in 1995 with the focus on the Decade of Churches in Solidarity with Women. The exposure visits were organized at centres in Argentina, Brazil, Chile and Uruguay. The second week when participants all met together in Rio de Janeiro had the theme "Encountering Our Own Identity". Participants shared their experiences of the exposure visits and then reflected on the questions, "Who am I as an African, Asian, American, Caribbean or European?" and "where are the women; what are they doing?" The following week had the theme "Affirming our Identity" and looked at issues raised by the Decade in general, with a particular emphasis on the impact of the economy on women and on justice for women. There was also a presentation and discussion on women's hope through theology. For the final week, the theme was "Women Working for Empowerment" with the opening question, "What can we do?" Participants then spent three days considering appropriate strategies for empowerment. Bible study and worship were woven throughout the three weeks that were spent together.

In CLLTs, the learning process is built on encounter. There is the encounter in the exposure visits and the encounter between the other participants. The visits often take participants to contexts radically different from theirs. For a few days they are able to enter into the life and work of their host community, not just observing but feeling the differences of ways of life, styles of work and articulations of faith. Particularly in the case of global CLLTs, where participants come from different regions, the exposure may be both exciting and disturbing. Removed from surroundings where even great difficulties can be faced in a setting that is familiar and predictable, participants may experience a sense of vulnerability. The participants also encounter one another in the small groups that undertake the exposure visits and in the larger gathering of the full course. From the composition of the small groups to the planning of the process of the whole month, every effort is made to provide opportunities for interpersonal engagement across the variety of ethnicity, context, confession, gender, personality and experience.

Experience, exciting or threatening, by itself does not necessarily result in learning. It is one of the recurrent themes of this book that we have to create opportunities for reflection to be able to deal with our experiences. CLLTs use a variety of methodologies to enable learning to come from experience. In the course of the exposure visit there are opportunities for participants to try to make sense of what they see of and feel about the context and one another. When participants all come together, they interact with one another through discussion and creative activities rather than receiving input through formal presentations on the theme. The whole process is dialogical rather than instructional. For that to be effective, space has to be created in which people feel able to take risks in opening themselves up to others.

In CLLTs, learning takes place in and through four kinds of community – the community that hosts the participants' exposure visits, the community of the institution where the residential component of the CLLT takes place, the community of the small group in which each participant shares the exposure visit, and the community of all the participants in the residential component. The interactions that take place are not only between individuals but also within these communities. There is collective and individual experience, sharing, and learning. Participating in a CLLT builds up an understanding and experience of teamwork. Participants also may have an opportunity to explore the development of community in which a conflict arising from difference is not sim-

26

ply managed but where the gospel concepts of repentance and reconciliation become meaningful.

The aim of a CLLT is not simply to give individual participants an experience of ecumenical education for their own benefit. The people who attend such courses are all in a position to use what they have learned when they return home. Of course, one would always hope that they can use what they have learned about the content of the theme. I want to stress, however, that the most important thing they can take home with them is good practice, not in the sense of trying to replicate a CLLT in their own situation, but in those elements that I have tried to draw out as being particularly significant in the process. The only justification for such a considerable investment of time and other resources on behalf of both the organizers and participants is that the latter return home as evangelists for creative ecumenical education. They should be inspired to preach this message, not by telling people about it, but by their own good practice of it.

Ecumenical education is about the transformation of relationships, understandings, attitudes and actions. The testimony of participants over the years confirms the CLLT as a good example of creative ecumenical education:[1]

"Everything was shaken up... I came away from this experience convinced more than ever of the essential catalytic importance of [laity] centres helping in the creation of a more just and peaceful world."

"My participation in the CLLT... was an exposure that also changed my attitude towards many things... My target is to train many agents of transformation and renewal in the church in particular and the society at large."

"This global consciousness I received for the very first time and it never left me."

Even more interesting than these and many more tributes like them are the lists of participants in various courses. I can see many names of those who have been or still are deeply influential in their own contexts and in the global ecumenical movement.

"Towards a Feminist Pedagogy" – a workshop

We move from reflecting on a particular form of ecumenical education to an example, a specific event. I have chosen it because it made a difference to my own thinking and practice. The workshop, held in 1997 in the Philippines, came out of the work of the WCC on justice, peace and creation. This work indicated that any understanding of education is incomplete without the perspectives of women. Not surprisingly, the majority of participants were women, with only a handful of men.

The workshop was held to probe various questions. How do women perceive and interpret reality? What is their vision? What can we learn from all this? If there were a distinctive feminist pedagogy, what difference would it make? In describing this workshop, I do not want to concentrate on the answers that came to these questions but rather on the process by which we engaged with them.

Participants had been asked to prepare by writing an account of our life story in terms of particular struggles, the impact of significant milestones, our notions of power and identity, and changes in our self-understanding. We also were asked to write about our experiences in education: evaluating our experiences, identifying values and principles, considering the impact of approaches used and identifying sources of hope.

When most us attend courses or workshops we are used to being given a timetable of activities and to entering a room that has been set out and prepared. Even if we recognize that it might be necessary to change the programme slightly as it goes along, we expect to be able to know what we will be doing on Thursday at 3 p.m. It gives us confidence that the organizers have thought the event through and planned properly. This workshop began with no set timetable, other than meal breaks, and an empty room. This approach was rather disconcerting to those who thought they knew how to run a workshop even though, in fact, it was all carefully thought through. It was up to the participants to fill the empty space.

The first activity of the workshop was to make the empty space a place, the participants' place. Multicoloured pieces of cloth were hung on the walls. Around the edges of the room people displayed pictures, books and literature representing their work. A focal point was created on the floor in the centre of the room with flowers, a bowl of water, a Bible and a candle. As we sat around, it became the centre of gravity for the whole dynamic of the workshop. It grew during the week as we added symbols of our lives and our work together. Around it we sang, prayed, moved, told stories, talked, cried, comforted and, in the process, learned. It was a place where we could be ourselves and we could be together.

We placed life at the centre of the workshop. The opening worship included participants sharing symbols they had brought with them. One by one, a mother and child statue from Kenya, a Zapatista doll from Mexico, a basket from Zimbabwe, a woven cloth from Finland, a holding cross from Australia and many other symbols were placed at the focal point. Each was an item of interest in itself but more important were the personal associations that gave them symbolic value. Over the course of the workshop, other symbols were added – flowers, leaves, stones – each representing a story or thought from our time together. Life was also place at the centre by participants telling personal stories, some with laughter, others with considerable pain.

From the life stories, the conversations moved naturally to trace the roots of common struggles, suffering and pain for women and to reflect on the cultural values, religious traditions and historical conditions that shape women's lives. We reviewed our experiences in education, identifying trends and key elements and exploring the nature of women's accumulated knowledge and experience. The distinctively feminine elements that the workshop included were the significance of life stories, healing and dealing with the subjective aspect of education.

In my own reflections on the experience of this workshop, I noted some important elements in addition to those already described in the example of CLLTs. The first is the importance of personal preparation. Any kind of learning is more difficult if we enter the experience unprepared. It is commonplace for educators to say that we must build on people's prior learning and experience. The workshop asked participants to arrive prepared by having already reflected on their own life stories and their educational experiences, the raw materials from which the learning process was created.

Ecumenical education is not about *us* creating space where *they* may learn. On the basis of what I have described we could see it as learners taking empty space and making it their place – a safe, creative place for learning, a place marked by their symbols of life and faith.

Telling life stories was a significant way of learning about ourselves and with others. Clearly, for some, it was a therapeutic process in itself or from the response of the hearers. Story-telling and healing became closely linked. A transformational education must contain elements of healing. But story-telling raised questions about how we listen, honour, respect and empathize with the person without imposing our story on her or him.

The ecumenical movement, like the churches, often buries itself in words, often as a way to avoid feelings or action. Creative ecumenical education can benefit from the symbol, the touch, the movement and even the tear. Our discourse does not always have to be with words.

There is also something to be learned from something that did not work in this workshop. One of the participants was not able to attend for the whole time and attended for only one day. In trying to be helpful in moving our discussions forward, he suggested that we might try a mind-mapping exercise. He gave a very good demonstration of how it could work for us. Because he had not been on the journey so far with everyone else, his presentation felt intrusive and it failed to connect at some significant points.

The example of this workshop is not that we can just find a room and invite people to turn up and expect that ecumenical learning will happen. There is a difference between careful preparation and heavy structuring. In many ways it is easier to draw up a tight programme and stick to it. That could be a kind of ecumenical education, but it wouldn't be very creative!

Congregational partnerships and exchanges

As a child in Sunday school in Ipswich, England, I gave my pennies for the work of Baptist missionaries in places like the Congo (now the Democratic Republic of) and India. I had pictures of the schools, hospitals and churches I helped support. In spite of changes in my understanding of the theology of mission, I still retain a particular feeling from my childhood for a select group of countries in the world.

For many of my counterparts today, their relationship with other countries is more focused. The congregation to which they belong may have a relationship with another congregation in Africa, Asia, Eastern Europe or Latin America. They may exchange e-mails and letters sharing news and will certainly feature in one another's prayers. Groups of people may pay visits to gain more direct experience of the life of the others. Sometimes the relationship is at a different level in the church. Dioceses or local synods may be linked, with mutual visiting more likely to be on the agenda.

This development appears to be a move in a good direction. Instead of children and adults learning about the work of missionaries in a distant country, with both the context and the activity seen through Western eyes, they can relate directly to the people of that country. It seems to be a great opportunity to learn from one another. Congregational partnerships and exchanges should be fertile ground for ecumenical education. Two recent studies – one originating from research done in Germany and the other from the WCC – have affirmed the potential of such partnerships and relationships. Both, however, raised questions about their effectiveness in practice. Although the studies considered many issues around partnerships, I will draw from them only what seems to be of significance to ecumenical education.

There is a strong tradition of direct partnerships between German and African parishes or church districts. These have been analyzed in some depth and set against the historical development of the understanding of partnership in mission.[2] The research describes visits to the African churches as having crowded programmes of visits to congregations, sometimes several in one day. The German visitors experience warm welcomes and joyful worship but have little opportunity to engage with the reality and meaning of the daily life of the African people. On visiting Germany, the African visitors' programme is also packed full and also includes visits to church institutions and congregational groups. There are also visits of a general cultural nature. African visitors are likely to be asked to talk about their work and context. I had the impression that the Europeans wanted to learn about the Africans rather than engage in a mutual exploration. The research looked at changed attitudes in individuals that were a product of the exposure, at whether these changes affected the inidividuals' behaviour, for example to people from different cultures, and at whether these changes in individuals affected the collective attitudes and behaviours of the congregations of which they were members.

There seems to be no doubt that many individuals find such visits a significant experience but, as I will keep emphasizing, experience does not automatically produce learning. There is a telling sentence from a WCC publication that seems to say it all: "The opportunities for ecumenical learning arising from such visits are, however, barely put to use."[3] There is little time or desire for reflection with members of the host community or, most surprisingly, among the group of visitors.

These partnerships offer an experience that the ordinary tourist will never have – the opportunity to share people's lives by living in their homes and entering into some of their activities. Yet at the same time the research draws attention to an inherent barrier to learning. Visitors are received as sisters and brothers in Christ in a harmonious relationship. Opportunities for reflection and evaluation that deal with what has been seen, experienced and felt in the course of the visit will reveal just how foreign we may be to one another.

The fear of conflict may encourage both sides to remain at a superficial level. The fear of change also may inhibit both the host congregations from learning from the visitors and the congregations of the visitors from accepting the implications of what has been learned by their representatives.

The research warns against making partnerships and exchange visits simply an educational exercise. I would agree if this means that such visits are not just the raw materials for a glorified seminar. But I would also want to say that learning is of the essence of the ecumenical movement and of Christian faith. Partnerships and exchanges must always been seen as educational.

The German research raises four important issues:
- There is a need to keep economic and other disparities from preventing a learning encounter between equals, an encounter aimed at mutual learning and change.
- All involved have to learn how to communicate across cultures, otherwise encounters will come to nothing or even reinforce prejudices and stereotypes.
- Attention needs to be paid to how what is learned can be shared and applied in a different context, particularly the congregation.
- Learning will not happen unless there is an intentional making of time, opportunity and appropriate processes for reflection.

Encounter learning

The Education and Ecumenical Formation team of the WCC undertook a study to find out how far encounter learning promotes ecumenical attitudes.[4] Its methodology involved distributing questionnaires through the WCC constituency, and two face-to-face consultations in Africa and Asia. Not surprisingly, much of what has emerged resonates strongly with the German research. There are some interesting outcomes, however, that are helpful to our discussion here.

The principal difficulties reported with encounter learning can be summarized as:

- the financial and other resources necessary for visits to happen, which limits the experience to a select few;
- The need for more careful orientation and preparation on both sides;
- communication in terms of both the languages spoken and the differences of culture;
- a lack of time for full immersion and for reflection;
- the dominance of a financial discourse where one community has needs and the other has resources;
- confusion around the implications of ecumenism for the churches and for ethical, environmental, economic and political issues;
- uncertainty as to what to do with the experiences of visits in terms of learning and future action.

The positive comments made centred around the experience of encounter. Words such as "awareness", "understanding" and "relationship" were used frequently. My own feeling is that although all that is good, it does not represent the kind of fundamental change in attitude and behaviour, i.e. transformation, that I hope would be a mark of true ecumenical education for individuals and congregations. It is quite possible to understand more and to be more aware without changing anything.

The research indicates that while there are a large number of North-South relationships, there are very few South-South relationships. There is no mention of North-North relationships, although I know from my own experience that these exist. This suggests that our understanding of such partnerships is limited to the transfer of resources, which would explain the frequency of North-South as against South-South partnerships. When I say that most of the North-North partnerships of my experience are wealthier congregations or parishes assisting those in deprived areas in the same country with human and financial resources, you will see that they fit my explanation. Yet the challenge of ecumenical education is to learn together. We cannot give justice to those who suffer injustice, peace to those for whom there is none or

God's promised fullness of life to those whose lives are empty. We have to learn these things together. Perhaps the biggest challenge of ecumenical education is to learn how to learn from one another and then to learn with one another.

One final insight from the research is the importance of immersion. The problem with many partnership and encounter programmes is that visitors become spectators of the drama of other people's lives and faith. They observe and, if given the chance, may reflect on what they have seen and heard. I do not want to undervalue the potential of that for transformation. To be immersed in another community, however, is to have a different level of experience. In a world of short courses and quick results, the time and commitment demanded for this kind of immersion does not make it a popular option. The other word for immersion used in the research is incarnation!

You and I

You may feel the opportunity to participate in anything like these examples will never come your way. That is OK. I did not intend to offer a prospectus so that you can sign up for an ecumenical education experience. Nor do I particularly want to encourage you to go out and organize something similar. I use the examples to draw out some important features of ecumenical education that you might apply in a whole variety of ways.

We don't have to cross oceans or even cross the road for an immersion experience. We already are immersed in a community. Our daily lives are full of encounters with other people. Most of us live in communities that have always been religiously and culturally plural or have recently become so. The people we encounter in the street or at work may be of another Christian tradition, may be of another world faith, may not be part of any organized religion or may give no meaning to faith at all. Most of us do not have to walk far to encounter the "other". Unless we are racist, fundamentalist or xenophobic we can see that our lives are rich with such experiences.

Ecumenical education is much more than opening our eyes to what is around us locally and globally, but that is a starting point. The stories in the gospels of the blind being given sight are as much about being able to see, as in understand, as anything physical. In later chapters, I will suggest why we are blind to the opportunities for ecumenical education that are close to hand and how we can help ourselves learn.

The issue is what we do with these kinds of experiences. I have drawn from the other examples the need to make time to reflect on our experience in order to learn. Our problem is that neither our schooling nor our Christian nurture may have equipped us to do this. Ecumenical education needs to be done in community. I have come across a few congregations that have created opportunities for their members to reflect together on their everyday encounters. The setting may be denominational but the experience from which to learn is widely ecumenical. It seems to me that this is what church should be about. Our worship, our praying, our mutual care and our service in the community should place our daily encounters in dialogue with the "givens" of our faith. Then we will learn and be transformed.

NOTES

[1] Mithra G. Augustine, *History and Hopes of CLLTs*, Geneva, WCC Education and Ecumenical Formation, 1999.
[2] Lothar Bauerochse, *Learning to Live Together: Interchurch partnerships as ecumenical communities of learning*, Geneva, WCC Publications, 2001.
[3] *Ibid.*, p.144.
[4] Gert Rüppell ed., *Ecumenical Learning in Partnerships and Exchange Relations: Study Process on Congregational and Church Experiences: Report on Initial Findings,* Geneva, WCC Education and Ecumenical Formation, 2001.

3. Breaking the Boundaries of Thinking

Try this exercise. Take a sheet of paper and mark on it a grid of nine equally spaced dots like this:

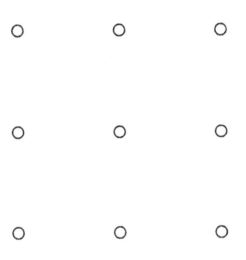

Now take a pencil and draw four straight lines so that every dot lies on at least one line. To make it more complicated, your pencil must not leave the paper.

Like all such problem-solving puzzles, the answer is easy, once you know it!

Draw the first straight line from left to right joining the dots in the top row. Do not stop at the third dot, but continue to the right for a distance equal to the gap between the dots.

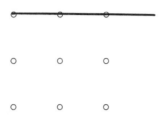

Draw the next straight line downwards, diagonally to the left. Then go straight up and finally diagonally down to the right.

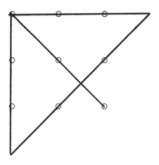

Like most people, when I first attempted this puzzle, I failed to find the answer. Once you know the solution, it is interesting to watch other people trying to work it out. At first, people tend to take a starting point such as one of the dots at a corner of the grid. Once that fails, they often try other dots as starting points. The point is, very few envisage using the space *outside* the grid.

Something about the symmetry of the dots persuades the eye and brain that the area is enclosed. It is as if we had drawn a picture frame around the area in our minds, joining the outer dots, then told ourselves that the solution to the puzzle must be in the framed area.

Trapped in our own thinking

Why should we narrow down the area in which we search for a solution in this way? Forming what can be called a *frame of reference* is a habit that our minds learn to be able to cope with life. To make immediate sense of a constant flow of physical, mental, emotional and spiritual experiences, we each develop our own frames of reference and use them to incorporate or reject interpretations of life. Without a frame of reference, even the supremely effective human brain would be unable to cope with all the incoming sensory information. This exercise of joining dots with lines provides a simple illustration of the way our inner frame of reference often influences our perceptions and ultimately our understanding. It also demonstrates that such habitual thinking may prevent us from thinking and acting creatively.

When I first began to drive, a car would have a handbook containing a problem-solving chart. Following the steps in the chart enabled you to quickly discover why the engine would not start so that, hopefully, you could put it right. You did not have to begin by thinking about how the internal combustion engine functions and working out a solution from first principles. It was not necessary to think deeply, just to answer the questions. This solved most problems. If it was something more complicated, then the skills of a mechanic were required.

In the same way, some of us turn to a medical dictionary when we are feeling unwell and test our symptoms against those of particular diseases. It can be reassuring to discover we only have the 'flu or, of course, we can wrongly convince ourselves that we have some serious illness. These kinds of checklists or problem-solving charts are rather like frames of reference. They save us from taking time or having the knowledge to begin from first principles. For the most part, they are very valuable but occasionally they are misleading and will lead us to a wrong diagnosis and action.

When you meet someone for the first time, you do not knowingly work through a checklist to discover whether you feel positively or negatively about him or her. You don't stand there consciously reading the other person's body language, looking at his or her appearance, listening to how he or she speaks and so on. But you probably do this without realizing what is going on in your mind. You will have built up a frame of reference based on things such as your values and your previous experience of other people. You don't have to stop the conversation to analyze your reaction to the other person, nor do you have to spend time thinking about what you like or dislike in other people. If the information from your senses matches a positive frame of reference, you will like the person; you may even experience love at first sight! Occasionally you may find yourself deceived by a preliminary positive response or find that as you discover more about the other person you feel more positively towards them than you did initially.

A frame of reference is created from our life-time experience of feelings, sensations, associations, concepts, values and responses. The two most significant influences are the culture in which we live and our earliest care-givers. Our frame of reference is a structure of the assumptions we build up in order to understand our experiences. That which fits a frame of reference is incorporated into it. That which fails to fit is rejected as irrelevant, mistaken or deviant.

Thus an inner frame of reference is an essential shortcut to understanding the world, one adapted and evolved over thousands of years to enable humans to respond quickly to events. Thanks to socially formed frames of reference, we save valuable time in understanding how to respond in terms of our thoughts, emotions and actions to each particular event encountered in every day life. Without it, we would live in constant confusion. As I hope to demonstrate, however, our frame of reference also can restrict our thinking if it is not expanded through learning.

To return to our problem-solving puzzle, when the solution lies outside our frame of reference we may first label it impossible or decide that there is an error in the instructions. But if the solution is provided, we will probably incorporate it into our frame of reference because it is innocuous and does not threaten our basic thinking. Indeed, the next time we are confronted with such a puzzle we will probably look for solutions of the same kind.

Frame of reference

There are two dimensions to our frame of reference – the first relates to our habitual ways of thinking. One common habitual way of thinking applies the "like me" or "like us" test that we apply to other people. We measure them against our own values, attitudes, ideas, beliefs and behaviour. In one single thought this may separate us from those who differ in ethnicity, gender, sexual orientation, religion, class, political philosophy and so on. We do not need to know anything about these people other than the fact that they are different from us. We may never personally have encountered any one individual in each category. We may see those who fail this test as enemies, as people to be condemned for their beliefs or life-style or simply as those not worth noticing.

The second dimension to our frame of reference relates to our point of view. In contrast to the "like me" test, it is much more specific and may vary with time and context. Nevertheless, it is still a means of instantaneous judgment. Although we do not necessarily recognize that we have this way of thinking, it is very powerful and resistant to significant and sudden change. On the positive side, it acts as a stabilizing influence on our thinking. Unfortunately, it also means that it is easy for us to live with no way of challenging our misapprehensions. Even when someone is confronted with information or an experience that, to an observer, would totally undermine a particular aspect of thinking, it persists in the face of the evidence.

I can give an illustration of this from my previous experience as a university chaplain. Take a student with an understanding of the Bible as the word of God that implies that the Bible must, therefore, be internally consistent, that each part of the Bible says the same thing. This may have been reinforced by the selective biblical basis of the preaching and

Bible study in the person's local congregation. This person goes to university to study theology and encounters for the first time the rich diversity of the Bible. Faced with the evidence that the Bible is not internally consistent and that the inconsistency can be viewed as a positive thing, what does the student do?

Some, of course, broaden their frame of reference in this respect. Many, however, hold on to their more powerfully shaped view and adopt strategies of self-justification in order to maintain it. One such strategy is to regard university study as an academic game that you play according to the rules to win your degree, but you go home to play the game of faith according to different rules. It would be easy to caricature this as intellectual dishonesty, but that would be to misunderstand the problem. Such dishonesty would be a deliberate act of the will. What I am suggesting is happening here may not be as calculated as it is not overtly recognized.

Although it is not as well researched, it seems that what we have said about individuals also can be said about communities. There are collective ways of thinking that we become accustomed to for much the same reasons. It is said that the former British prime minister, Margaret Thatcher, once claimed that there was no such thing as society, only individuals. Yet as I observed events in Britain, she had no qualms about utilizing a sense of nationalism, collective habitual thinking, when it suited her own ends.

Christians develop their own habitual collective thinking. We can see this in the existence of denominations and traditions within the church. At the same time, it can develop across denominations. The ecumenical movement would be one example, the charismatic movement another. We need to be very careful neither to claim God as the origin of our habitual collective thinking nor to blame God for it. Every movement of the Holy Spirit, as, for example, both the ecumenical movement and the charismatic movement could claim to be, may transform collective thinking or be distorted by it. Sometimes both happen at the same time.

Implications for ecumenical education

Our frames of reference are a problem for ecumenical learning. As we have seen, it is not because our frames of reference are somehow evil. They are useful to us on an everyday basis. But they may predispose us to reject or find it difficult to accept what lies outside our current range of experience and the ways in which we interpret life and faith. Part of our intention in ecumenical education is to develop a frame of reference that is open to the other person, to a different way of believing and acting; to be open to learning from them rather than reacting against them.

What does this imply for ecumenical education? My first thought is that prevention is better than cure. As I have indicated, accustomed ways of thinking are notoriously resistant to change. We need to begin with the Christian nurture offered to children in the home and the faith community. It is here that the framework of thinking begins to be erected. Children need to be exposed to multiple perspectives if they are to grow up with an openness of outlook. We need to continue the process with adults. If we have the experience of looking at situations and events from different points of view, we are less likely to adopt explanations that are oversimplistic and one-dimensional.

This poses a real challenge for Christian education where it has been tightly tied to a particular tradition as locally experienced. Even ecumenically produced resource material that attempts to offer a broad vision of the faith can be limited in its impact by the way it is used in a local congregation. Churches, like all human communities or institutions, have a vested interest in maintaining the status quo. Thus churches also have a vested interest in education that domesticates (instils conformity) rather than liberates!

An even bigger challenge was identified at the consultation "At the Frontiers... "held in October 2000 in Bangkok, Thailand. The WCC invited representatives of the world faiths to reflect on religious education. The participants suggested that state schools and faith communities should teach faiths other than that of the student. Religious educa-

44

tion in one narrow tradition often supports the misapprehension, suspicion or even demonization of those who believe differently. Even when this is not the intent, it tends to happen. The challenge for Christian congregations is to give in their Christian education a positive and sympathetic view of their neighbours of other faiths. One good reason for this is the promotion of communal harmony. If we do not challenge evil stereotypes, we are complicit in the communal violence that feeds on false myths about the other faith community. There is also another powerful reason for learning sympathetically about other faiths. It is a means of understanding and deepening one's own heritage of faith. This runs counter to the usual objection that if children or adults are exposed to other faiths, it undermines their own.

The positive view is easier to understand if we appreciate the value of having more than one perspective on anything. Let me explain by using an illustration. Imagine a fish swimming in a glass fish tank in someone's home. Pretend that this fish has powers of sight and thought akin to humans. The fish can know the fish tank from its experience of swimming in it. It knows its boundaries and the geography of the sand and rocks on the floor of the tank. It can see that there is a world outside the fish tank and may be able to observe some of its features, though not clearly because of the nature of water. Yet the fish can have no idea of what its fish tank looks like or of its relationship with the rest of the world. An internal perspective cannot reveal that. Understanding requires an external as well as an internal perspective.

Encounter

If we want to take ecumenical education seriously, we must work to help churches become learning communities rather than domesticating communities – to have broad or multiple perspectives rather than a single, narrow view of their faith and the world. Being realistic, that will not be enough. We have to find ways in which we can break out of our constrained ways of thinking. We will look at some techniques for doing this but first, I want to remind us of one important concept that we have already noted.

The concept can be summed up in one word, "encounter". When we encounter the "other" – the other person, the other way of thinking or believing, the other way of describing life, the other way of celebrating, the other way of worshiping, the other way of doing – we are given an opportunity to break out of our accustomed ways, our frames of reference. It is only an opportunity because the experience may do nothing at all for us. Worse, it may actually allow us to confirm our worst stereotypes.

Encounters happen in a variety of ways. We meet other people all the time. Because of the way human life tends to structure itself, we tend to meet mainly those people who are like us. However, even in our neighbourhood, school, work and church, there is likely to be a range of differences in politics, in beliefs and so on. These people, perceived as friend or enemy, are as rich a resource for our personal learning as we are for them. Yet we make no space to reflect on what these encounters say to our context and us.

Other encounters are more deliberate. We may visit people on another continent in connection with our work or as part of a relationship between different churches. We may attend a global meeting where people are drawn together from a wide variety of contexts. In the ecumenical movement, we have sometimes given the impression that all we have to do is bring people together and something will happen. If we want proof that this is not the case, the recently published study of congregational partnerships between German and African churches, referred to in the previous chapter, clearly shows this. The exposure and encounter that happened as groups visited each other did not always produce any ecumenical learning. In short, the reason for this is that those involved were given little opportunity to process their experience so that it changed their perceptions. Many were just left with traveller's tales but no greater wisdom.

Breaking out of habitual thinking

It is difficult, if not impossible, to break out of habitual thinking on our own. It is a far more complex process than simply an act of will. We can open ourselves to multiple perspectives and to encounters with others but still remain within our set ways of thinking. I have identified one need, the opportunity to reflect on our experience. I am convinced that practice is another need.

If you play a musical instrument or a sport, it helps to practise. We have various words to describe it – "rehearsal", "exercise", "training". The essence of it is that we can try things out in a situation where is does not matter if we make mistakes. We can try out different ways of doing things and we learn as much from what does not work as from what does. We keep going until we know how to get things right in the most effective manner. We need to practise thinking differently in situations where we can learn without harming anyone else or ourselves.

I have always had a great suspicion of books that offer ten easy ways of doing this, that or the other. At the same time, there is a fascination about them. If only there were a magic formula that worked every time, we all could be successful, influential, rich and famous. What I offer here are not simple or easy ways; there is nothing magical about them. All I can say is that they appear to me to be based on sound principles and that I have seen them work. They are all based on groups of people meeting together and learning together to break the boundaries of habitual thinking.

Brainstorming

Brainstorming works best when there is a well-defined issue or problem but the way forward is not self-evident. It allows the generation of a large number of related ideas and thoughts from which we can learn how to act. One idea can spark another. Brainstorming is a participatory exercise for a group of people and enables them all to feel involved and responsible for the end results.

It usually begins with a group of people sitting together where they can see words or phrases written up on paper or on an overhead projector. People are asked to suspend judgment and just produce ideas, however strange or impractical. I have found it most effective to begin by giving everyone a few minutes to think about the issue being considered. Then when group members give responses, everyone is likely to be able to offer something. We can either write up ideas as they come or keep going round each member in turn. Words and phrases are written up without comment until the flow stops completely.

Although brainstorming has considerable potential to help us break out of conventional thinking around issues, it often does not deliver. There are many reasons for this and it is essential that we are aware of them. The following are some helpful suggestions to make brainstorming more effective.

– Brainstorming works best if the issue is narrow and focused. Thus, "How can we make the world a better place?" will only produce diffuse ideas. Something more specific such as, "How can we work together to reduce violence on the streets of our community?" could produce ideas for activity.

– Allow sufficient time. The first responses almost always represent conventional thinking. There's nothing wrong with that, but you do not need to have a brainstorming session to surface these ideas. It is when the thinking goes beyond our commonplace solutions that it gets interesting. Even when the initial flow of ideas dries up, give people time for further thought, perhaps sparked by what is already written up.

– Ask participants not to offer judgments on what they hear. This immediately kills the process. Comments such as "that wouldn't work here" or "we tried that before" and "that's a great idea" or "you've got the answer" are unhelpful. Brainstorming is not about winners or losers. Everyone must refrain from judging negatively or positively and keep an open mind. Fresh thinking requires totally open minds. This requires sensitive but firm facilitation.

– Value people's contributions equally. Brainstorming should not become a competition between the quick-witted members of the group as to who can produce the most ideas. Creative thinking can come from the person who offers many thoughts but, equally, it may be the person who only says two things who opens up something new. Everyone should have the opportunity to speak and everyone's contribution should be acknowledged.

– Encourage people not to fear offering way-out or odd ideas. People may be inhibited where the facilitator is in a position of power or authority, since different thinking may be contrary to their personal or official stance. They also may fear the reactions of the others in the group. The facilitator must be neutral and give no opinion on what is offered, only encouragement.

Brainstorming is not principally about finding an answer or solution. It is a step towards that answer. The goal of brainstorming is to create alternatives. The greater the number of ideas, the greater the likelihood that the final choice or answer will be successful.

Having several large sheets of paper filled with words or phrases is of little use in itself. It is probably most helpful to look for examples of the same thought expressed in different ways and for links between ideas. Depending on the size of the initial group, it can be helpful to get participants to do this in pairs or triplets. This encourages everyone to be involved in synthesizing the results of the brainstorming.

You could end up with a long list of items that combine everything that emerged from the brainstorming. It can be helpful to ask for brief comments on each item and then ask every member of the group to choose, say, the five most significant. When the choices of the whole group are brought together there is an immediate indication of which are worth in-depth consideration.

An alternative approach would be to draw a map of the relationships between the ideas that have been produced by the brainstorming. The basic problem or central issue is placed at the centre of the map and ideas branch out from it.

It may be necessary to keep redrawing the map until you are satisfied with the way it represents what you have said. I have drawn the start of a map that could have been produced from a brainstorming exercise on the issue I used as an example.

Here is how we might begin to "map" ecumenical education:

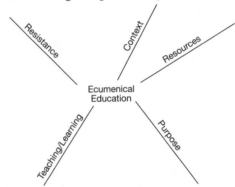

Then here is how two of the branches might start to develop:

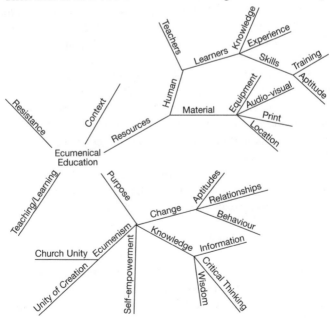

As a visual means of organizing your thoughts, concept mapping or mind mapping is an excellent and creative tool. It is beyond the scope of this book to include any detail but there are many resources in print and on the World Wide Web to help you explore its potential.

Simulations and role-plays

Simulations and role-plays help us enter situations and explore what they mean in safety. We can try different solutions and ways of behaving, knowing that our actions will not hurt anyone. Play for children is not simply a pleasant diversion to pass the time until they are grown up. It is a powerful means by which they are able to try life out in safety. We have discovered that it can be equally powerful for adults when they enter into the spirit of things.

As I see it, the difference between a simulation and a role-play is that in a simulation, you are yourself and, in a role-play, you take on the character of another person. By introducing the problem or issue dramatically, we can involve the whole person, including our imagination. We can appreciate other points of view from the inside. It is the freedom from the constraints of being your responsible self that creates the opportunity to break out of conventional thinking.

There are different benefits from both approaches but the following points will help avoid failure.

– Clearly define and explain the situation and people's roles within it. As with brainstorming, the more focused the problem or opportunity is, the more effective the exercise will be.

– Try to help participants overcome their self-consciousness. Such exercises work best within groups of people who know and trust one another enough not to worry about appearing foolish. Even in such groups the facilitator must encourage active and imaginative participation.

– Encourage participants not to confuse the exercise with reality. What is said and done in a simulation or role-play is not real, but people may still feel hurt. Part of the work at the end of the exercise should always be for people to leave it behind and resume normal living. As part of the learning process participants should express how they felt in the course of the exercise but not carry those feelings with them. Again, the facilitator has to be sensitive in dealing with this.

– Choose a situation that corresponds to or relates in some way to the participants' contexts. If it does not, they have difficulty in seeing any need to take the exercise seriously.

– Make what has been discovered explicit. It is not enough to give people experiences; we have to provide an opportunity for them to create new meaning from them.

Case studies

A case study is a group exercise that examines an account of a situation or problem. In many ways, case studies are similar to simulations or role-plays without the dramatic involvement. They tend to go into more detail and thus may sharpen analytical problem-solving skills. The information about the case study can be presented well in advance of the meeting of the group so that participants can do some initial reflection and research. It is possible to share what actually happened and get group members to compare it to their analysis and suggested action.

As with the other techniques, the full potential of case studies may not be realized if the following guidelines are not followed.

– Present the information in sufficient detail to allow in-depth reflection.

– Choose case studies with care and with the knowledge of the participants' situation. Participants need to feel that the case study has some relation to their own experience.

– Help participants see this as more than an intellectual exercise, so that their reflections will be in-depth and committed.

– Allow sufficient opportunity for participants to reflect on what has been learned through the process and content of doing the case study.

Brainstorming, simulations/role-plays and case studies are simply three activities through which we can practice breaking out of habitual thinking. Their great advantage is that they are communal activities and will develop collective, as well as individual, creative thinking.

There is a significant difference between the big idea of encounter and the techniques I have described. Encounter is direct and personal, whereas the techniques all rely on stepping outside of ourselves and our context to free up our thinking. One is real, the other is artificial. One is dangerous, the other can be done in safety. Although these techniques and others can be very helpful, in the end I believe that encounter is what is necessary.

Conclusion

In writing about the need to break the boundaries of learning, to broaden our mental and spiritual frame of reference so that we can escape from the restrictions of our habitual ways of knowing, I am not just thinking of people who are peculiarly narrow minded. I am thinking of myself, who also needs to broaden my frame of reference. I, too, need to break free from my pre-prepared responses that prevent me from seeing new possibilities.

Ecumenical education is not only about learning the history of the ecumenical movement or learning how to use the insights of a significant ecumenical document such as *Baptism, Eucharist and Ministry*. It is about opening and transforming the way we perceive and respond to all of life. It is about a change of attitude and behaviour. Unless that happens, we will only have stories to tell about the ecumenical movement but will have gained no greater wisdom.

4. Learning As the Essence of Faith

> Remember yourself ten years ago. How have you changed over those years? In particular, what has changed in your personal beliefs, your spirituality and in the way you live out your values?
>
> What has caused these changes, or why do you think you have remained as you were?

Many years ago I was standing at the door of a church shaking hands with the departing congregation. I had been the guest preacher at Sunday worship. I had been inspired by something I read in the WCC's *One World* magazine to preach on the different images of Jesus we may have and how we can benefit from seeing Jesus through other people's eyes. Instead of the usual thanks for a "nice sermon", an elderly woman took me to task. She told me she had had the same image of Jesus all her life. It was one given to her as a child in Sunday school. It had maintained her faith through some very difficult times. She believed we should stay with what we are taught.

As I reflected on her comments, two thoughts came to mind. First of all there was, for her, the tried and tested value of a faith in Christ handed on to her in childhood. I wanted to share in her gratitude for that. At the same time, however, I felt a sense of sadness. There could have been so much more. We do not need to deny the value of our original learning in faith, as a child or later in life, in order to affirm that there are always greater riches to be discovered, more resources in faith for us to draw on and a wider vision to be unveiled. Ecumenical education is a means by which we can discover the "so much more" of faith in God.

In 1620 Pastor John Robinson preached a farewell sermon to the pilgrims who were leaving England for the freedom of the "New World". A first-hand account of the sermon by Governor Edward Winslow in *Hypocrisie Unmasked*, 1646, records Robinson offering the hope and the challenge that the Lord had more truth and light yet to break forth out of his holy word. Robinson complained of the state of the

Reformed churches, saying they were unable to go beyond that part of God's will discerned by Luther or Calvin. "They stick where he left them, a misery much to be lamented," he said.

Robinson's positive thought was picked up by the hymn writer George Rawson in the 1850s, who left us with this verse from his hymn "We limit not the truth of God to our poor reach of mind".

> We limit not the truth of God to our poor reach of mind –
> By notions of our day and sect – crude partial and confined
> No, let a new and better hope within our hearts be stirred
> For God hath yet more light and truth to break forth from the Word.

For *a new and better hope*, ecumenical education is not an optional extra. In the course of my work, people often remind me in encouraging kind of way that ecumenical education is vital to the ecumenical movement. Naturally, I have a vested interest in agreeing. However, there is more to be said. I tried to express that in the title of an article I once wrote: "The Ecumenical Movement in the Service of Ecumenical Learning". Ecumenical education does not simply perform the same task for the ecumenical movement that school systems are required to do for society. Rather, the ecumenical movement is, although not exclusively, the place where individuals and communities learn how to be and to act. Learning is not one of the activities of the faithful, but is of the essence of Christian faith.

Learning from the Bible

Learning from one another has always been the experience of the churches. The diverse group of women and men who met for prayer following the ascension (Acts 1:12–14) had already had an intense learning experience through their involvement in the ministry of Jesus. The snatches of conversation between the disciples recorded in the gospels and the significantly different interpretation of Jesus in each gospel suggests that even at the birth of the church there was the potential for learning from each other. It is not simply the case, however, that the Old and New Testaments record many examples of learning experiences that can encourage present-day believers. The message seems to be that learning is of the essence of faith. We tend to use the word "disciple" in the sense of being a follower and forget its root meaning from the Latin "discere", to learn. Faith is dynamic, implying constant learning, and not a static state where all answers are known.

In looking at biblical examples of learning as a paradigm of faith there are two powerful motifs – journey and encounter. It is as we travel together that we learn. The new experiences shared on a journey prompt a communal and individual learning. Likewise, encounters with those who are different from us challenge our self-understanding.

To begin with the motif of journey, the story of the exodus dominates the Old Testament. Among the many ways of interpreting this story is to see it through the lens of learning. Liberation came as much from what the people learned together on their journey as from the physical escape from slavery in Egypt. The story describes three particularly significant and interrelated aspects of learning.

They learned who they were. It was not just the Egyptians who forgot who Joseph was and why the Israelites were in their land. The first chapters of Exodus are a reminder of the way in which dislocated and oppressed people can forget their identity. The Israelites came only to know themselves as slaves. The group's self-image was so powerful that when things became difficult at the start of their journey they complained that they would be better off in the "normality" of slavery (Ex. 14:10–12, 16:1–3). In the course of the exodus they claimed or reclaimed their identity as people of God.

They learned who God was for them. The loss of identity was related to the atrophy of the memory of the source of that identity – the God of Abraham, Isaac, Jacob and Joseph. The story describes Israelites calling out to the Lord in their misery. That is no more surprising than many contemporary post-Christian fellow citizens who in moments of crisis will turn to a God who is all but forgotten in their daily lives. Even Moses had to be convinced who God was. It was no sudden awakening of faith in the God of Abraham, Isaac and Jacob that led to the start of the journey out of slavery, but the persistence of Moses and Aaron. The rediscovery of God came as they travelled. It is interesting to note that the journey begun but not completed by Abraham, another foundational story of the people of Israel, is also initiated by a call from a God who was only dimly apprehended (Gen. 12:1–9). The exodus journey, like all such journeys, is the difficult process of coming to faith in God.

They learned how to live in community. The part of the exodus story described in Leviticus and Deuteronomy could be caricatured as a list of rules and regulations that seem to make little sense to readers in the 20th century. As slaves, the Israelites lived by their masters' rules and for their benefit. They had lost the art of living in their own community. Thus we can see these rules and regulations as exemplifying the attempt to work out how a just and healthy community could function. Liberation comes from being set free *and* in learning how to live together in freedom.

The story of the Israelites once they had arrived in the promised land contains a warning to those who would only see the journey as an image for a process of learning that is a means to an end. A feeling of having "arrived" is the prelude to disaster. Time and time again the people of Israel forgot what they had learned about their identity, about God and about how to live in community. It was only as they were in travelling mode again, either metaphorically or literally by exile, that the learning process was restored and there was salvation or health for the community.

In the gospels, the call of Jesus to the disciples was "follow me". For them, following Jesus meant leaving a settled existence and living with the uncertainties of life on the road. The gospels include several accounts of the conversations Jesus held with the disciples as they made their way from place to place. They witnessed the healings and listened to the teaching and the stories. The disciples discussed everything from how to pray to who was the most important. Jesus took time with them to reflect on why things had gone wrong. For instance, while Jesus was on the mountain for the transfiguration, the rest of the disciples failed to help an epileptic boy (Matt. 17:1–21). Jesus even gave them direct experience of doing his work and then engaged with their experience on their return (Luke 9:1–10).

Jesus' example

The journeys with Jesus were potential learning experiences for the disciples. Jesus recognized this and on occasion expressed frustration that the disciples had seen and heard but not understood (e.g. Mark 7:18, 8:14–21). They had been making the physical journey and probably had been making an emotional journey, too. However they had not travelled far in the kind of learning for which Jesus was looking.

It is usual for Christian writers on education to refer to Jesus' teaching style in responding to those who came to him with questions. In the context of demonstrating that learning can be seen as a necessary Christian paradigm, it is more instructive to look at the way Jesus himself learned through encountering the "other". This will be controversial for those who understand Jesus to be so "at one with the Father" that he knew everything and, consequently, had no need to learn.

The writers of Matthew and Luke and the subsequent editors of the New Testament were quite radical in preserving the accounts of the encounter between Jesus and the Canaanite or Syrophoenician woman (Matt. 15:21–28 and Mark 7:24–30). The woman approached Jesus to ask for her daughter to be healed. According to these accounts, Jesus strongly resisted her request on the grounds that his mission was only to the people of Israel. However, the woman's faith in Jesus caused him to change his mind. In this encounter with a person whose gender and ethnicity made her a culturally unacceptable counterpart, Jesus learned about his own mission. I can only describe this as ecumenical learning!

Journey and encounter come together in the Acts of the Apostles. It was as the gospel travelled out from Jerusalem that the early followers of Jesus learned what it meant to be Christian. The story told in the Acts of the Apostles is of the opportunities for learning from each other's experience and of the barriers to such learning, as the followers of Jesus were driven out into the wider world by persecution and the Spirit. In spite of the positive encounters between Jesus and a Roman centurion (Matt. 8:5–13) and the Syrophoenician woman (above), the movement out from Jerusalem began as a Jewish mission. It took encounters with Gentiles and the work of the Holy Spirit (e.g. Acts 10:1–48) for the early Christians to learn that "God has given even to the Gentiles the repentance that leads to life" (Acts 11:18b).

We need to remember that what we now read in the New Testament as the "givens" of Christian faith began as pieces of learning in response to events, individuals and communities. The correspondence found in the Epistles between Paul and young churches he had helped to establish or had visited gives an example of people exploring who they are, who God is and how they can live together in community. Again it can be argued that problems arose in these early Christian communities when they began to feel that there was no more to be learned, that they knew all they needed to know.

In both the Old and New Testaments, faith is a dynamic concept. We see learning happening by individuals and community. Ecumenical education must stand in that biblical tradition.

Understanding human development

Learning is about the process of moving on in faith. We cannot think about learning as the essence of faith without taking into account the work that has been undertaken in recent decades on faith development. It owes a great deal, sometimes quite directly, to the work of developmental psychologists. As the whole idea of faith development may be unfamiliar, I will sketch out where these ideas come from and the implications for seeing learning as the essence of faith.

For much of human history people have been categorized into children and adults. The division between the two, usually marked by a rite of passage, has been at an age appropriate in a particular culture for the child to take on adult tasks and responsibilities. Apart from the obvious changes of physical growth and degeneration at either end of the age spectrum and of language development in children, the two states tended to be regarded as static. A child was a child and an adult, an adult.

The idea of psychological development in children was popularized by Jean Piaget, a Swiss psychologist. In his published work beginning from the first part of the 20th century, he identified four stages in the mental growth of children. The child starts with the physical control of objects (birth to two years), moves on to the development of the verbal skills of naming objects and intuitive reasoning (age two to seven), on to dealing with abstract concepts such as numbers and relationships (age seven to 12) and finally begins to reason logically and systematically (12 to 15). Piaget's research in developmental psychology had the goal of explaining how knowledge grows. It is not simply that children know more the older they get. The way in which they are able to learn, to process knowledge, develops over time. Children's logic and modes of thinking are initially entirely different from those of adults.

Many questions have been raised about Piaget's work. Whether or not there are four discrete stages as he defined them need not concern us here. The work of developmental psychologists who have built on or challenged his work have established that children's ways of thinking develop from birth to adulthood. As we will see, this includes religious development.

More recently, we have come to see that adulthood is not a static state either. Adults change as they grow older. We recognize the physical changes in ageing in ourselves and in our friends. Perhaps, though, it is not so obvious that there is also a developmental process through adulthood. Many people who now accept the development of children as self-evident require convincing of the case for adult development. Some developmental psychologists have suggested an

ordered progression for adults akin to that developed by
Piaget for childhood. Others see development as contextual
and, therefore, not able to be described as a linear process.
Some indicate a movement towards clearly defined goals
such as becoming a fully integrated person. Others, seeing
development as a dialectical process, describe the goal as the
constant interaction between person and context.

To help us think through ecumenical education in relation
to adult development, I offer two examples of the results of
research in this area. Both offer an account of stages through
which adults move in the context of a developmental scheme
for the whole of life. As we will see, each was produced on
a very different basis.

American developmental psychologist Robert Havighurst
suggests six stages of development, the final three relating to
adulthood.[1] The stages are age specific and related to the typical tasks that mark them. In the thirty years since Havighurst
produced his theory, there have been significant changes in
Western society that mean the exact ages and tasks may no
longer reflect reality. For many cultures, the tasks may never
have been entirely appropriate. For our purposes, those do
not matter too much since I am introducing this for its way
of understanding adult development rather than the detail.

In summary, Havighurst's stages of adult development
and their typical tasks are:

Early adulthood (18–35)
- selecting and learning to live with a marriage partner;
- starting a family and rearing children;
- managing a home and getting started in an occupation;
- taking on civic responsibility;
- finding a congenial social group.

Middle age (35–60)
- establishing and maintaining an economic standard of living;
- assisting teenage children to become responsible and
  happy adults;

- achieving adult, civic and social responsibility;
- developing adult leisure time activities;
- relating to one's spouse as a person;
- learning to accept and adjust to the physiological changes of age;
- adjusting to ageing parents.

Later life (60+)
- adjusting to decreasing physical strength and retirement;
- adjusting to the death of a spouse;
- establishing an explicit affiliation with one's age group;
- meeting social and civic obligations.

Havighurst suggests that there should be a link between these tasks and learning activities for adults. He speaks of "teachable moments". Either the tasks themselves or the need to move on to the next stage offer both opportunities and requirements for learning. They also offer us an analysis of the personal context of learners in terms of their preoccupations.

Eric Erikson, an American psychologist, proposed eight stages of development over the life cycle, each representing issues that have to be resolved.[2] He put them in the form of opposites in tension. Erikson described three stages of adult development but deliberately left open the exact ages at which they occur:

Young adulthood. The tension is between intimacy and isolation. Intimacy is the ability to be close to others, as a friend, a lover and as a participant in society. This requires a clear sense of identity without the need to prove yourself. Intimacy is not the same as promiscuity where the closeness is too casual, without depth and commitment. There is the danger of exclusion when you isolate yourself from others and exhibit negative behaviour in compensation for your loneliness. This stage enables you to carry with you psychosocial strength Erikson calls love.

Middle adulthood. The tension is between generativity and self-absorption.

Generativity is a concern for the next generation and all future generations and therefore is less self-centred than the previous intimacy. There is no necessary expectation of reciprocity. Generativity is not only expressed through having and raising children but also through teaching, writing, invention, the arts and sciences and social activism as a means of contributing to the future. The self-absorbed person is not a productive member of society. This stage gives a capacity for caring for others.

Older adulthood. The tension is between integrity and despair. Despair comes through endings – for example, of employment and through death of others – and decline in capacities. Integrity means coming to terms with your life and its ending. This stage offers the capacity for what Erikson calls wisdom.

Although there are similarities with the task-related analysis of Havighurst, Erikson's stages have a different basis. Erikson suggests that, although stages build on one another, it may be necessary to return to previous stages to complete unfinished work on resolving that tension or to produce a new resolution because of a significant change in life, for example, bereavement.

It may help you to pause and reflect on what you have just read.

Looking at yourself and at people you know, how far do Havighurst and Erikson reflect what you observe? What tasks or tensions would you want to list under different stages?

Where do you see a religious dimension to the tasks and tensions?

What insights do these analyses of adult development give for education, especially ecumenical education?

There is another way of looking at adult development that comes to us from studies on women's development and on feminist pedagogy, or teaching. It is not divided into stages since it emphasizes that we are constantly being formed as persons through relating to others. Its key elements are relational and collaborative learning, with an emphasis on empathy for others.

In introducing and illustrating the idea of development throughout the life cycle, I have tried to do three things:

– to introduce description and analysis that remains unfamiliar to many people

– to show how this is useful for the educator in terms of understanding the variety of personal contexts of learners at different times of their lives and of working with them in ways that relate to their concerns, preoccupations and developmental needs

– most importantly in a chapter on the inextricable link between learning and faith, to prepare the ground for a more specific discussion of the development of faith, especially with an ecumenical dimension

The development of faith

In recent years attention has been paid to the development of faith, either under the general influence of the interest in human development or, more specifically, drawing on the results of research. Faith often has been seen as something that may develop in terms of religious knowledge or depth of relationship with God. In that case, learning may be useful to faith but not of its essence. If faith has the same dynamic as other significant aspects of ourselves as persons, we can expect to be helped by a description and analysis of the development process. To help our reflection on this, we will look at two very different examples of faith development theory, each of which takes a significantly different approach.

To describe the development of faith, American theologian John Westerhoff makes use of the image of a tree. When a tree is cut down we can tell its age by the number of rings in the wood of its trunk. Each concentric ring represents a growing season. We can even tell how good the conditions for growth were for each year of the tree's life. From his observation of people in churches, Westerhoff identifies four styles, not stages, of faith. They are like the rings in a tree trunk. The styles grow out from the centre and remain pre-sent.[3]

In brief outline, the four styles of faith are:

Experienced faith: Faith is initially formed through the direct experience of trust, love and acceptance. This holds true whether you are a baby or an adult who comes new to the Christian faith. In conversation, it is being related to which is significant rather than the nature of theological language used.

Affiliative faith: A sense of belonging is created through religious stories, experiences of awe and mystery, feelings and experiences. You identify with the faith community and act according to its norms. There is an uncritical acceptance of belief and religious practice. Although there may be deep commitment, it is to what others offer rather than to what is owned by you. Many people do not grow beyond this style of faith.

Searching faith: This is the style of faith where the faith that has been received comes under critical analysis. It is about questioning, doubting, experimenting with other ideas and exploring alternative spiritualities. Although it is essential in the process of development, it is uncomfortable for both the individual and the faith community.

Owned faith: This is a mature faith that expresses itself in personal integrity and social action. You are able to both stand up for what you believe and be open enough to listen to other points of view. New meaning is found in and through story, symbol and ritual. Owned faith is enriched and further developed, rather than threatened, by the challenge of different perspectives on the truth.

Westerhoff's four styles of faith resonate strongly with ecumenical education. The end point of development is an owned faith that is both self-confident and open to others, one that values and draws on resources across the spectrum and one that is socially active. It is the result of a critical consciousness working on what has been given. However, it is the community of faith that is the primary nurturer. For Westerhoff, this is located in the congregation as the crucible of worship, witness and service and in the home. Educational programmes are at best adjuncts to the experience of participating in the faith community. For ecumenical education, this immediately presents us with a problem. Few congregations are thoroughly ecumenical. It means that we have to develop ecumenical community or to broaden the ecumenical vision of denominational congregations in order to have effective ecumenical education. That is a significant challenge, as educators often prefer to create new curricula than create learning community.

The other challenge for ecumenical education is the observation that most people do not grow beyond the affiliative style. Perhaps the churches prefer it that way! We could see Westerhoff's searching style of faith as the development of critical thinking. This ought to be an aspect of the Christian nurture offered in local congregations. Instead, all too often, restricted and conservative ways of thinking are formed. Ecumenical education cannot operate in a separate world from the churches. The clear implication of this is that churches that wish to see themselves as part of the ecumenical movement must pay attention to what is learned in the local congregation and Sunday school.

Stages of faith development

In the 1970s and 1980s a wide-ranging research project in the United States opened up faith development as a stage process. James Fowler directed the research as professor of theology and human development at Emory University, Atlanta, Georgia. The image Fowler uses is that of a life journey. As we saw earlier, the image of journey is significant for us. We pass through a sequence of stages, but many will never reach those towards the end. Faith, which is not understood to be the same as belief, is something active and has to do with our relationships with other people and our world as well as with God. Times of crisis can be a catalyst for moving on to the next stage but occasionally may cause us to return to an earlier stage.

Fowler's titles for each stage are rather difficult to comprehend, so you will find in the brief summary that follows alternative titles that have been suggested by various commentators.[4]

Stage 0: Primal faith/the incorporative self (alternatively nursed faith or foundation faith)

We gradually distinguish ourselves from others.

We experience love and care.

We begin to form relationships and learn to trust or mistrust.

Stage 1: Intuitive/projective faith (alternatively chaotic faith, unordered faith or impressionistic faith)

We move away from total dependence and imitation.

Stories help us make sense of the world.

We are unable to separate fact and fantasy.

Rituals are important for us and we take symbols literally.

Stage 2: Mythic literal faith (alternatively ordering faith)

We are aware of belonging to the faith community.

We adopt the stories, practices and beliefs of the faith community.

We begin to be able to tell the natural from the supernatural.

We probably still think of God in human terms.

Stage 3: Synthetic/conventional faith (alternatively conforming faith)

We try to understand the world and ourselves.

We tend to conform to religious authority.

We become aware of different conflicts and claims.

Some may not progress beyond this stage.

Stage 4: Individuative/reflective faith (alternatively choosing faith or either/or faith)

We take on responsibility for our life-style, beliefs and attitudes and do not merely reflect the understanding of the group.

We can express ideas in abstract terms.

Many never reach this stage.

Stage 5: Conjunctive faith (alternatively balanced faith, inclusive faith or both/and faith)

We are committed to our own position while respecting the viewpoints of others.

We feel empathy and show active concern for all.

We learn to live with contradictions and tensions.

It is unusual for people to reach this stage before mid-life.

Stage 6: Universalizing faith (alternatively selfless faith)

We love life but hold it loosely, taking it seriously but not too seriously.

We experience the kingdom of God as a reality.

This is the most complete stage of union with God in human life and only a few saints reach this stage.

It is tempting but unhelpful to compare Westerhoff and Fowler. The points of similarity relate to the fact that both focus on faith in the Christian community. There is little in common between the actual approaches. Questions have been raised about whether Fowler's work implies that there is a difference in the value of faith as people move through the stages. It is difficult to talk about progress through stages without implying an increase in esteem. Fortunately, God's love is indiscriminate.

Fowler himself does not make excessive claims about his stage theory. It is a working model. Whatever the difficulties associated with a stage theory, it has the value of emphasizing the dynamic nature of faith and the lifelong nature of its development. This is another indication that learning is of the essence of faith.

If we accept Fowler's stages of faith as a working hypothesis, it can be argued that it is not possible to move beyond stage three with its characteristic of conforming to religious authority without an ecumenical dimension to learning. Stages five and six (for the few who reach them) represent some of the desirable outcomes of ecumenical education. The general thrust of the development, however, is towards greater personal benevolence. Ecumenical education should encourage a greater socio-political involvement in working against all that prevents humanity from experiencing fullness of life.

The importance of community

There are two areas where I cannot be fully satisfied with stage development theories for faith. The first is that they only deal with the individual. The faith community and the global and local communities are the context within which the individual develops his or her own faith. Both Fowler and Westerhoff have important things to say about the necessity of involvement or full participation in the faith community but it is to the benefit of the individual. The question not addressed is the development of the faith of the faith community. This is both more than and different from the faith development of the individuals that comprise it.

My sensitivity to this point arises from my reflection on being part of a Baptist tradition. It can be argued that the emphasis on the baptism of believers among a dissident group of Christians in the 17th century was a means of identification with and commitment to a covenanted faith community. We now have the position where most Baptists see baptism as primarily a personal profession of faith. The emphasis has moved from the community to the individual. Given the current emphasis in society on individuals realizing their potential and on the individual as a consumer, this shift in understanding of baptism may be understandable, but for me it is regrettable. One value of ecumenical education for the churches may be the recognition of the community aspect of faith in belief and action. Certainly there can be no individualistic ecumenical education.

The second area of my concerns about stage development theories for faith relates to the difference between transition and transformation. Educators frequently discuss how we can help people move from one stage to the next. It is not always clear what the factors are that make for transition, but we try to identify them and then produce learning activities to assist. In relation to ecumenical education, this may miss the point. Ecumenical education may not be about moving people on by incremental steps. It may be more about transformation, which I would see as a more fundamental event in terms of change. Perhaps opposing the two is a false antithesis, but it serves to remind us of the radical nature of change we require, which may not be achievable by transition.

Conclusion

The different forms of description and analysis of human development in general and of faith in particular can be useful tools for understanding ecumenical education. We must be careful, however, not to let them control our thinking or the way in which we view people.

It is possible to see the business of learning as that to which Christians are called. Whatever our status within the church as baptized, confirmed, commissioned or ordained, we are called to be learners. I believe that whenever we think that we know all there is to know about the Christian faith and that we have no more to learn, we are profoundly mistaken. The end of the journey is the kingdom of God, which, according to the images presented by Jesus in the parables, is itself a dynamic rather than a static state. The signs of the kingdom that are realized within the lives of individuals or communities in the process of learning are encouragements to move on. Ecumenical education, particularly that which involves encounters with people who are different from us, is not a chance to make everyone more like ourselves. It is an opportunity for something new to emerge in us and in them.

Learning is not only that which helps faith develop nor an important activity in the practice of faith. Learning is of the essence of faith.

NOTES

[1] See, for example, Robert J. Havighurst, *Developmental Tasks and Education*, New York, D. McKay 3rd ed., 1972.

[2] His principal works are: *Childhood and Society*, New York, W.W. Norton, 1993, *The Life Cycle Completed*, New York, Norton, 1998.

[3] See John H. Westerhoff, *Will our Children Have Faith?*, New York, Morehouse, 2000.

[4] My summary of James W. Fowler, *Stages of Faith: The Psychology of Human Development and the Quest for Meaning*, San Francisco, Harper & Row, 1995.

5. How We Learn Together

Think of something you learned in the past few days. You might have learned it at home, at work, in a leisure activity or on a formal course; where you learned it doesn't matter.

What difference does what you learned make to you?

The woman had been a lay leader in a local congregation. One day the pastor had come to her and suggested that she might like to leave and join another church. Why? She asked too many questions about the faith and this was unsettling for the newer members of the congregation. As I listened to her tell this story, I kept to myself the thought that if anyone was threatened, it was the pastor. This was an extremely painful story for her to tell. What surprised me most on hearing it was, unfortunately, not that this incident had taken place but that the woman still wanted to have anything to do with the church.

Enquiring minds are not always welcomed. There is an English saying that "a little learning is a dangerous thing". In other words, a slight acquaintance with a subject can delude us into presuming an expertise we do not have. It implies that the more we learn the better. I would say, however, that any process of learning is potentially a dangerous thing!

Transmission or transformation

I understand learning, especially that encouraged by ecumenical education, as a process of transformation for the learners and their context. This is in contrast to the learning seen in many church and state educational systems as being limited to adding information and skills through a process of transmission. With transformation, learners develop the ability to reflect critically on themselves and their contexts. With transmission, the learner may be passive and unreflective.

Much of my own experience of education involved accumulating knowledge and reproducing it to the satisfaction, or not, of examiners. Even in church, we had an annual scripture exam for children and adults, and the fact that it was produced ecumenically did not improve it! It was a great revelation for me to discover the possibilities of critical thinking.

When universal education was being developed in the West, a process in which the churches played a significant role, there were many points at which basic education for all was resisted. It was feared that teaching ordinary people to read and write might encourage them to think for themselves. Education was necessary for the ruling classes. As for the rest, they simply needed to be able to function efficiently within the role that society allocated to them – a utilitarian view of education that still permeates Western thinking. The desire to preserve the status quo is an aspect of the self-preservation instinct of all human institutions, including those of the churches and the ecumenical movement.

Paulo Freire, one of the most significant educators of the 20th century, had to leave Brazil because the process of education he developed was too threatening to the state. His literacy programmes not only equipped adults to learn the technical skills of reading and writing, they also enabled them to take back responsibility for their lives. In exile, he worked as a consultant for the WCC. There are interesting accounts in the WCC archives of the puzzlement and resistance of church people to the idea that such education could be liberating in their situation.

Freire's book, *Pedagogy of the Oppressed*, took on almost cult status and influenced the thinking of a whole generation of educators. I chose the word "thinking" deliberately as I am not sure whether the influence on practice was very deep or long-lasting. I remember attending a university lecture on Paulo Freire. The lecturer spoke warmly of Freire's challenge to systems of education that passed on second-hand knowledge without developing critical consciousness. He seemed to be unaware of the irony of doing this in a style that was contradictory to Freire's approach. Freire's work became an object of study rather than an example to be followed; exiling someone is not the only way to quieten a disturbing voice!

Education is welcome, or even becomes a priority, when it is designed to improve the effectiveness or efficiency of our work or to increase knowledge within the institution's own self-understanding. Yet despite the many fine words on education pronounced by institutions from governments through to churches, processes of learning that may threaten the status quo or the concepts on which it is constructed are not really welcomed. The divisions of the church are a sad testimony to our inability to be institutions that are able to cope with new learning. Using this analysis, the pastor in the opening story was behaving in an entirely predictable manner.

There is an interesting contrast between the attitudes of Jesus and those of his followers. Jesus worked with questions. He responded to all those put to him by genuine enquirers and by trouble-makers. His answers, often in the form of a story, provoked the questioner to coming to his or her own judgment and, where necessary, breaking the boundaries of current religious thought. The question "Who is my neighbour?" produced a story and a question that took the original listener and future readers right to the heart of the issue (Luke 10:29). It forces us to have to decide the answer for ourselves, not only in the context of the story but also in our own behaviour.

Unfortunately, Jesus' followers then and now have not always behaved in such an open manner. For example, the stories Jesus told to get people to think for themselves have had correct interpretations attached to them, sometimes written back into the gospels. The reader or hearer is no longer encouraged to engage with the story but only to receive a given meaning. Jesus was willing to take the risk that people might get it wrong. He was not an enforcer of a narrowly stated truth, but the liberator of hearts, minds and spirits.

Apologists for the ecumenical movement have sometimes argued that ecumenical education is no threat to the churches. They are right. If there is any threat, it does not come from any process of *ecumenical* learning but from learning per se. Bible study or exploring our Christian tradition does not have to be labelled ecumenical to make it disturbing or threatening to churches as human institutions! We should be realistic about, but not disheartened by, institutional resistance to open and creative learning.

We all learn, but it's not all good

We learn far more that we are ever taught. We acquire most of what we learn throughout our lives in an informal manner or incidentally to other activities. Some of the most fundamental learnings come without sitting in a classroom or taking a course.

Two examples come immediately to mind. We learn our mother tongue through being immersed in a language environment. The more people talk to us, even before we can talk, the greater the quality and quantity of our language learning. We have to recognize as well that language is not just a medium by which we communicate, it influences, if not controls, the structures of our thinking. In this case the effects, positive and negative, of this early informal learning can last for the whole of our lives.

The second example is the way we develop the values by which we live. Our values affect our behaviour and attitudes. In spite of the calls of those who demand that people should be taught "right and wrong" through formal educational processes in schools and religious communities, values are acquired informally through participation in communities that are significant to the person. The primary place values are developed is the home. As children grow into adulthood, other influences on values include peer groups and religious communities.

The influence comes not from the stated values of, for example, the family or the church, but from the practised values. Our problem as parents is that what we tell our children is good and right is not necessarily what we practise ourselves. What churches proclaim about the love of Christ is undermined in practice by bad relationships between members of a congregation or between different branches of the church. One of the gifts that children bring to family or church life is that of seeing such inconsistency. Unfortunately, when children point out our adult inconsistencies to us, we rarely take them seriously enough to change our behaviour. It is a sad reflection on our moral development that becoming an adult seems to mean developing the skill of self-justification. Informal learning can be self-serving.

Our religious language

One of the things you learn as you grow up is the name of the language you speak. The name of the language is of little significance until you recognize that there are people who speak other languages and you need to differentiate yourself from them. I grew up in a Baptist congregation, so my religious "language" was Baptist. I learned that language through being in and around the worship and life of that congregation. I attended Sunday school but we have known for some time that in its traditional form, Sunday school is only likely to add to the information we have rather than shape our belief.

The denominational label only became significant when I learned that there were other Christians who were not Baptist and there were, indeed, people who were not Christian. In discovering through informal learning that the religious language I spoke was Baptist, I was profoundly mistaken. To continue the language analogy, Baptist is a dialect of Christian, not a completely different language. By that, I mean that all that is held in common across the church in terms of belief, doctrine, values, worship and service is stamped with a denominational label. From inside the local congregation you have no means of knowing that it is not all exclusively yours.

I have had the opportunity to lead worship in many different denominational congregations and the following experience is representative in a minor way of what I mean. At the end of worship in a Methodist church, someone congratulated me on choosing "Methodist hymns" even though I was a Baptist. I gently pointed out that all the hymns were also in Baptist hymnbooks and one of them was actually written by a Roman Catholic. It is easy to hold ignorance up to ridicule and that is not my intention here. How could anyone be expected to know differently when brought up in a congregation where everything, including common Christian possessions, had the denominational label stamped on it? Even more starkly, I have sat in an ecumenical discussion group where a Protestant member confessed that it was only during the course of the discussion that he realized that Roman Catholics believed in Jesus. Mutual ignorance, suspicion and even demonization are alive and well and will continue to be until we are active in promoting kinds of learning that are ecumenical.

There will only be limited potential for ecumenical education where the opportunities for informally learning common Christian ways of thinking and acting are non-existent or deliberately restrictive. The denominational context in which people find themselves may be deficient in that there is no conscious effort to promote a recognition of what Christians hold in common, even though it is accepted in principle. There sometimes also appears to be a deliberate policy to not allow any commonalty with other Christians. The effect of both is the same – people shaped by their community experience in a way that makes them resistant to any learning that broadens their horizons.

The significance of informal learning needs to be stressed because of the apparent pre-eminence of formal learning. For many people, learning is what happens in the classroom, the seminar room or the lecture theatre. Learning that happens informally or incidentally is hardly valued. Learning is given its meaning not so much by its methodology or its content as its location. The place of learning provides elements of control, regulation and validation that have become predominant in all sectors of education. The more prestigious the location, the higher the value that is placed on the learning.

For the past five years, I have observed the applications that are made to the WCC's Scholarships Programme. Many are requests for courses at prominent universities in the North without apparent regard to the appropriateness of the course for the student's context on returning home, nor, indeed, for the quality of the course – prestigious institutions are capable of offering inferior products! The opportunity for learning is valued according to where it takes place.

For ecumenical education, both informal learning and formal learning have a role to play and both should be valued equally. We should be careful not to build false distinctions between them but to recognize, as I argue later, that it is the quality of participation that is the telling factor.

How learning theories can help us

In reflecting on how we can do creative ecumenical education, we need to be aware of some of the theoretical accounts of how we learn. In presenting them here, I am not able to do more than give the briefest indication of their implications for us.

Constructivism

By reflecting on our experiences we are able to construct our own understanding of the world. To make sense of our experiences, we each create our own "rules" and "mental models". From the constructivist perspective, learning is the process whereby we adjust our mental models to accommodate new experiences.

As learning is a search for meaning, its starting points must always be those issues where there is the need to construct meaning. The ecumenical movement has sometimes given the impression that such needs are generalized – the unity of the church, economic globalization, violence – and has tried to organize ecumenical education that takes the broad issues as its starting point. A constructivist perspective instead points us to beginning with the felt, contextual need – for example, disunity in the congregation or between congregations, local economic effects or violence in the local community. It is by starting with what is real for people that we can begin to construct meaning. Effective learning begins with people's own experiences.

If the purpose of learning is to enable people to construct their own meaning, processes that encourage memorizing correct responses and repeating meanings received second-hand are not appropriate. Unfortunately, many courses on ecumenism take the approach of giving students the information about the history of the ecumenical movement and an assessment of the issues in a style that does not encourage student to construct meaning. It is possible to teach ecumenism without any ecumenical learning occurring. Ecumenical education is as much about new attitudes as is it about being better informed, so the opportunity for personal meaning making is vital.

Making connections and integrating knowledge is also essential. The construction of meaning requires understanding the whole picture as well as parts of it, and understanding parts in the context of the whole. One of the problems that plagues education at all levels is the division of knowledge into subject areas or disciplines. There may be good reasons in the management of learning in institutions for this to happen. It is also increasingly the case that the expansion of knowledge means that no one can know everything about everything, even within academic disciplines. This has two unfortunate effects, however – we are not encouraged to make connections between the pieces of knowledge we do have, and we are encouraged to think in compartments.

When I visit theological colleges or seminaries, I have two favourite questions to ask: How is your learning contextual, and where do you integrate all that you learn? I am too often disappointed that no serious opportunities are created for students to make connections between the different subjects on the academic curriculum, their own experience and what they learn through placements in churches. Ecumenical education by its nature must be integrative.

A constructivist understanding of learning implies building on people's prior knowledge rather than using a standardized curriculum. It emphasizes hands-on problem solving with a focus on making connections between facts and fostering new understanding in order to analyze and interpret information and experience.

Behaviourism

Behaviourism defines learning as acquiring new behaviour and focuses only on that which is observable. It does not account for every kind of learning as it disregards the internal activities of the mind. Basically, it says that if a reward or reinforcement follows the response to a stimulus, then the response becomes more probable in the future. It is easier to see how this operates in terms of encouraging simple behavioural responses in animals than complex human thought patterns and behaviours.

I mention it for one particular reason – the introduction of the idea of reinforcement. Positive reinforcement does not have to come as a physical reward. It also can be approving words or body language. We should never underestimate the power of approval in reinforcing behaviour in ecumenical education or any other form of learning.

Social learning theory

Social learning could be described as observational learning. To oversimplify the theory, people learn by imitating others with desirable characteristics. These may be superficial in terms of appearance and popularity or deeper in terms of character or capability. We reproduce the behaviour of those who act as models for us. By behaviour, we mean more than good or bad manners but everything that we do. The theory makes a distinction between acquiring the behaviour through remembered observation and reproducing it when there is an incentive to do so. That incentive is usually the expectation of positive reinforcement.

There is a complex interaction between people, their behaviour and their environment. People's behaviour can affect their feelings about themselves and their attitudes and beliefs about others. What a person knows and does is affected by his or her environment and vice versa.

This tells us that the social context for ecumenical education is a powerful determinant of the outcomes. For many people in the churches, those called to be bishops, moderators, superintendents and the like may provide models for behaviour. When people observe leaders who are unenthusiastic or antagonistic towards ecumenism, they will reproduce that behaviour. When they see those committed to ecumenism in ecumenical gatherings but following another agenda in denominational meetings, they also will behave as if ecumenism were a parallel, alternative track. This, of course, gives us the traditional "Which comes first, the chicken or the egg?" question. Do we change the attitude of leaders so as to provide a better model for people or that of people so they produce an ecumenically minded leadership?

In ecumenical education we must provide people with an opportunity and environment to observe and model the behaviour that leads to positive reinforcement. Because much of learning happens within social contexts, we must encourage collaborative learning.

Theories of the brain

A great deal of attention has been paid in recent years to the structure and function of the brain. Learning is the natural function of the brain. It is happening all the time, whether we are conscious of it or not. The question is not how to make learning happen, but how to optimize the brain's potential. These theories suggest that traditional schooling methods often inhibit learning by working against the brain's natural learning processes.

The innate function of the brain is to make sense or meaning of all the different flows of information from inside the person and, via the sense receptors, from outside. This meaning comes through the recognition and classification of patterns. The brain can perform several operations simultaneously. The part of our memory that relates to rote learning is the least effective for understanding. It is only efficient in exporting the information that came in.

The most effective learning comes through the greatest involvement of the whole person. It is unnatural for the brain to operate just on that which comes through the eyes or ears. This supports a learning environment that fully immerses people in an educational experience. Ecumenical education, then, cannot only be something that happens in the seminar room or discussion group. At least part of the learning has to be done by being active in a context. Learners need the opportunity to consolidate and internalize information by actively processing it and thereby making meaning. Feedback from reality is much more effective than that from authority figures.

There is a temptation for educators to simplify educational experiences so that focus is maintained and people learn the right things. Brain theories point us to complex, interactive experiences that are both rich and real as the most effective way of learning. The experience has to be meaningful to the learner in order to create the right state of alertness in the mind. That which is externally imposed or which appears to be irrelevant will not stimulate learning. Ecumenical education should not be like school or higher education where one can often be confronted with those who are learning because it is required.

Learning styles

People learn in very different ways. Each individual has a particular way of perceiving and processing information, her or his learning style. How much anyone learns does not have so much to do with how bright she or he is as with whether the educational activity is in tune with her or his particular style of learning. Different learning styles are tendencies rather than absolutes.

Learning styles can be classified in terms of different ways of perceiving and processing information:

Concrete and abstract perceivers. Doing, acting, sensing and feeling enable concrete perceivers to take in information. Analysis, observation and thinking enable abstract perceivers to absorb information.

Active and reflective processors. Active processors make sense of an experience by immediately using the new information. Reflective processors make sense of an experience by reflecting on and thinking about it.

Because abstract perceiving and reflective processing are the qualities most rewarded by traditional schooling methodologies, we need to look to a variety of other approaches to support all learners in ecumenical education. The traditional skills of analysis, reason and sequential problem solving should be complemented by the equal use of intuition, feeling, sensing and imagination. Ecumenical education can learn much from feminist pedagogy in this respect.

Ecumenical education does not exist in its own universe of understanding. We need to draw on the considerable amount of research that has been done on the human processes of learning. We have to bring our values and our objectives into dialogue with learning theory to produce practices that are consistent and appropriate.

But I'm not intelligent enough

The capacity to think is not what makes us human, but we would not be human without it. As human beings we are more than dispassionate mental processors. We all think in varying ways. Talk of ecumenical education should not make us fall into the trap of believing that the traditional academic approach to thought is the only legitimate or effective way of thinking. We need to break out of our habitual ways of thinking about thinking! The more complex our world gets, the faster the rate of social and technological change, the more we are required to think using all aspects of our being, including both rationality and emotion.

We are finding that the former ways of knowing, believing and behaving can no longer be simply and automatically applied. We cannot just blame this on those who raise searching questions about the truths we used to accept on trust. Scientific research which, for instance, opens up the genetic manipulation of everything that grows including ourselves presents us with ethical dilemmas that are new and to which there are no pre-prepared answers. In the political sphere, globalization raises questions of popular control and accountability if the nation state, to which Christians have a strange attachment, loses its relevance. In societies where traditional structures have broken down, we face the challenge of creating stable and affirmative relationships at the personal and communal levels. It is not just our old solutions that are inadequate, but our old ways of thinking. Transformation rather than change is required.

At the beginning of the book, I suggested that ecumenical education should help us become map-makers rather than map-readers. In the examples above we are certainly sailing on uncharted seas. It does not mean that we must act as though we believe and know nothing. We have to develop a style of thinking that enables us to place what we presently know and believe into dialogue with the issues and contexts that confront us. We are not entering a value-free or faith-free zone. In bringing these into conversation with the realities of life, we have to recognize that both our values and faith and our understanding of and response to the situation will change.

There may be those who think that it sounds rather dangerous for our values and faith. I would respond that any faith or values that cannot stand engagement with our reality are valueless. It is such engagement that ultimately resulted in what we read in the Bible and that has given us Christian values and faith. Ecumenical education needs to be concerned with such dialogical or dialectical thinking, otherwise it will not be creative.

If dialectical thinking is a significant aspect, does that mean that ecumenical education is basically an intellectual or academic exercise that is for the few rather than for all? The question is an important one. My immediate answer is that ecumenical education is for all, individually and collectively. However, this question contains two kinds of assumptions that raise questions of their own. There can be an assumption that the "academic" may be an interesting kind of game to play but that it is irrelevant to real life. There is a phrase in English "to take an academic interest in something" which implies that the interest is only in the mind and without any practical outcome. Serious and structured study is important and should not be dismissed lightly. Ecumenical education can be justifiably and appropriately academic (and theological!). But it cannot be only that.

The second kind of assumption is that the world of the intellect and the academic is only for the few. In many countries higher education has been for the few, not because of the lack of resources but as a matter of political will. Universities were for an elite based either on social class or meritocracy. Higher education in such countries is being expanded through creating more and larger traditional university institutions and through providing alternatives such as the British Open University, which uses distance learning methods and does not require formal qualifications for entry. This expansion of higher university has demonstrated that a far higher proportion of a population can benefit from higher education than was ever thought.

It is not just the school leavers who have gone on to university when their counterparts of previous generations would not have dreamed of doing so. Mature students who left school with no qualifications and entered higher education on the basis of life experience often have surprised themselves and their tutors by their academic performance. Yet in parts of populations there often remains a general feeling that higher education is "not for people like us" or that, with no objective basis, "I am not intelligent enough." People are often capable of much more than they or we may imagine. Ecumenical education should never cheat people of opportunity because of misguided views of the academic or of capability.

This is the point at which we need to reflect on intelligence as it is implicit in the above. In casual conversation we may describe someone as being very intelligent. We can mean several things by this: They know a lot, they are good at working things out in their head or they are quick-witted. Intelligence may make some think of the IQ scores that have been used to segregate students at school or to determine employment opportunities. We recognize intuitively that intelligence is a meaningful concept, yet find it hard to give it an agreed substance.

It is unhelpful to say that intelligence is what intelligence tests measure. There is more to any person's intellectual ability and potential than success in doing tests. Intelligence is about the ability of our brains to perform certain tasks. Psychologists debate the nature of those tasks and whether intelligence is innate or the product of interaction with a person's environment. As for the latter, it would seem that both have to be taken into consideration. We should also recognize that, unless we are brain surgeons, it is only the environment that can be changed.

For many years, intelligence was thought of as a single underlying ability centred on linguistic and logical-mathematical abilities. For cultures built up around education as schooling with an emphasis on what are described as traditional academic subjects, this is an attractive proposition, especially since it carries with it the handy measuring tape of IQ testing. Had the original researchers on intelligence come from another culture, I suspect they might have produced a significantly different theory.

Multiple intelligences

Since the 1980s, other views of intelligence have come to prominence. These allow for different kinds of intelligence and are of particular interest for ecumenical education. In 1983, American educator Howard Gardner suggested that the concept of intelligence had been too limited by testing logical and linguistic abilities. He argued for the existence of several intellectual competencies that could be used alone or in combination. Individuals could be talented in some areas but have little capacity in others. It is not appropriate just to call people bright, average or dull.

Gardner described his theory as multiple intelligences. At first he listed seven intelligences as follow:

- *linguistic:* sensitivity to language, ability to learn languages, capacity for purposeful use of language;
- *logical-mathematical:* capacity to analyse problems logically, perform mathematical operations and carry out scientific investigation;

- *musical:* skill in performance and composition, appreciation of musical patterns;
- *bodily-kinesthetic:* physical ability and skill to solve problems or create products;
- *spatial:* potential to recognize and manipulate the patterns of wide space as well as the patterns of more confined areas. Examples of the use of this ability would be a navigator or an architect;
- *interpersonal:* capacity to understand the intentions, motivations and desires of others so as to work effectively with them;
- *intrapersonal:* capacity to understand one's self, including desires, fears and abilities, and to make use of that.

Gardner reviewed his original proposition in the light of further research and the immense interest that was created. Many people, including myself, had proposed additional intelligences. In 1999, he considered three further intelligences on the basis of the objective criteria he had set for the original seven. Only one fully passed his test:

- *naturalist:* capacity to recognize instances of members of a species, to distinguish between species and to chart out relations between species. This also applies to the ability to categorize manufactured objects.

Gardner also examined the claims of a spiritual intelligence. This is the one that I would have wanted to see added. Spirituality has been written off by such as Sigmund Freud as some kind of aberration, a symptom of neurosis or psychosis. But after a four-year research project at Nottingham university, UK, David Hay and Rebecca Nye reported support for the idea that spirituality is biologically natural to humans. This, of course, does not prove that there is a spiritual intelligence and we have to accept that Gardner could not objectify it in relation to his criteria.

The third claim Gardner examined was that of existential intelligence. He defined this as "the capacity to locate oneself with respect to the further reaches of the cosmos – the infinite and the infinitesimal – and the related capacity to locate oneself with respect to such existential features of the human condition as the significance of life, the meaning of death, the ultimate fate of the physical and the psychological world and such profound experiences as love of another person or total immersion in a work of art."[1] In the end, he was not fully satisfied that this was another intelligence and only half accepted it.

Emotional intelligence

The relationship between reason and emotion has intrigued philosophers and theologians for centuries. Within the Christian faith there frequently have been divisions between those who see faith as a rational exercise and those who see it as an expression of feeling. Serious theology may be caricatured as "academic" and "scientific", rejecting everything that does not fall within the rules of those activities. People's own theology, especially in some evangelical and charismatic traditions, can equally be dismissed as being centred on emotional experiences and not subjected to any rational discipline. From the opposite side, those who adopt a rational approach to faith can be accused of lacking a real relationship with God. Thinking has been seen to exclude feeling. This has had the double effect of denying human wholeness and creating a two-class society in the churches – those who are serious thinkers about their faith and those who feel their faith.

Because emotions are nebulous and complex to measure, scientists have found them difficult to explain. Recent developments in neuroscience relating to the structures of the brain that deal with emotions and thinking have given us new possibilities of understanding this relationship. One of the outcomes has been the concept of emotional intelligence introduced by Daniel Goleman, an American academic in psychology and personality development.[2]

One of the key insights of emotional intelligence is that all behaviour has an emotional component. Without our emotions we would not be able to value anything, make decisions or feel close to anyone. We also need our thinking capacities to generate options for how we should behave. The most basic of the various emotional intelligence skills is emotional awareness. Without being aware of what we are feeling, we cannot begin to behave or think appropriately. Other skills include being able to empathize and develop relationships with others, to delay gratification in order to accomplish our goals and to resist negative influences. Emotional intelligence, therefore, is all about reason and emotion working together.

These different understandings of intelligence have several implications for ecumenical education. They remind us that logical-mathematical intelligence around which Western academic education has been built is not the only useful or valuable human quality. There are forms of intelligence – for instance, those to do with relating, feeling and developing values – that relate far more closely to the values of the Christian gospel and, therefore, need to be equally valued in ecumenical education. In order to offer an education that is holistic, we have to engage with all that people are and not only with their capacity for logical thought.

We also should be reminded that wholeness rarely occurs or can be developed in any one individual. Rather, wholeness is found in a community where all the individual potential is complementary. So from consideration of the individual, we are again led back to the community.

Learning in community

As we have seen in these summaries of theories, learning cannot be seen as something done by individuals in isolation from their environment and social context. Other research has paid specific attention to the structures of communities and how learning occurs in them. Among the issues emerging, the following are particularly important for ecumenical education.

People learn in, around and through the communities to which they belong. Most of us, particularly in the West, belong to several communities: family, neighbourhood, educational, work, interest/leisure, church and so on. Some of these communities have smaller groupings within them or are part of wider relationships. We learn within all the communities of which we are a part. In spite of the individualization of learning through schooling, learning is basically a social phenomenon.

At least part of what makes a community are the stories, experiences, languages, values, beliefs and ways of doing things that are common. We learn this knowledge through being a member in that community and participating in its life. We learn practical and relational skills as well as cognitive knowledge. Learning happens through doing rather than observing or being instructed. Good community empowers people because it enables them to contribute.

Churches have always recognized this in the Christian nurture they provide through the home and the local worshiping community. More formal learning took place in monastic communities. This model was reproduced in seminaries that provided the formation of ministers and clergy through a number of years of life in community, even for those parts of the church that were not inheritors of the monastic tradition.

Their intuition that learning happens in community was correct. In my view, however, the community that should be the primary location for the formation of ministers and clergy is the church in its societal context and not an artificial creation. The fact that the churches have had so many good and faithful ministers and clergy is more attributable to the work of the Holy Spirit than the educational system that produced them. We should not produce artificial community simply as an educational methodology. If ecumenical education does not take seriously the learning happening in communities where people already are, it stands little chance of being either ecumenical or educational.

I want to make a clear distinction between people learning in community as described above and the possibilities of communities being learning communities. It is something I mention several times in this book because I fear that when we talk of ecumenical education we only have individuals in mind. If there is a community dimension, it is that the community is a powerful educator and that we hope, by giving individuals an ecumenical vision and practice, to influence communities. There is nothing wrong and everything right with both of those.

Communities are more than the sum total of their individual members, and communities do learn. Things like values and culture are learned by communities through what is handed down to community members, what comes to them from outside and their own experiences. In the context of this book, communities may be discussion groups, local congregations, national churches, councils of churches, ecumenical agencies and networks. These are communities of belief and intent and they learn.

To illustrate the point, a local congregation will learn how to behave in relation to its context. It may develop defensive or positive attitudes towards its neighbours, depending on the physical or psychological threats it perceives. It may focus its life on caring for its own members or on serving those around it. It may act as a predator or as a partner towards other Christian congregations nearby. Sometimes this behaviour is required by outside authorities or is generated by internal leadership. More often than not, though, it just happens. That is simply another way of saying that this community has learned a way of behaving, perhaps not explicitly or intentionally but learned nevertheless.

Learning that just happens in a community becomes problematic when it develops attitudes and behaviours that are at odds with its stated values. There has been much discussion in recent years about institutional racism. An organization may be racist in its behaviour and attitudes in spite of having strong official policies against racism. This does not appear to be connected only with how many people working in the organization are or are not racist. It is something that develops, is learned, by the organization as an organization. A local congregation may develop attitudes and behaviour that make a visitor who is not "like them" feel positively unwelcome in spite of a sign over the door proclaiming that Christ welcomes everyone. All of this is learned behaviour.

There are many who argue that communities and organizations cannot learn per se. Any learning that does happen is the sum total of the individual learning. My intuition is to remain with the discussion above and claim that ecumenical education should help communities as well as individuals learn. However, there are not yet well enough developed theories of community or organizational learning from which we can draw.

Because much community learning tends to be accidental, we have to find ways of making it more intentional. One of the motivators for individual learning is cognitive dissonance, that is where we recognize two things that do not make sense to us and so have to change one or the other. A very simple illustration would be that I believe that Christians never lie. My friend who is a Christian tells me something that I discover to be a lie. I have to learn either that Christians sometime do tell lies and perhaps think up some rules for when untruthfulness is permissible, or that my friend is not a Christian. The motivation for community learning could be intentionally examining our actual attitudes and behaviour against what we proclaim. The danger, as history often shows, is that communities, including church communities, are just as likely to change their stated values to justify their behaviour as vice versa.

Discussion, debate, dialogue and conversation

The best key for unlocking community learning that I have seen comes from writings about the nature of our discourse in community.[3] There are several words that we use to describe this – discussion, debate, dialogue and conversation – and it is worth examining what each one means. The root meaning of discussion is to scatter or shake apart. Think of words with the same root, such as percussion and concussion. The root meaning of debate is to beat down, that is, to do battle with words. Dialogue, on the other hand, is to draw meaning through. Conversation is to keep company with or even to turn together. I would not want to suggest that we have these meanings at the back of our minds when we

engage in these different styles of discourse. But it is significant that two very different styles are represented by discussion and debate, on the one hand, and dialogue and conversation on the other. The dominant style of discourse in politics, business and in other organizations throughout the
world is combative, where different ideas and understandings crash together, rather than collaborative, where understanding is clarified and deepened. The news media are complicit in this. A bitter political argument is a story; agreement
is not. Verbal confrontations so easily spill out onto the
streets as fighting.

My experience of discussion and debate in church circles
has all too often been of trying to score points and win, proving that I am right and you are wrong. Our styles of decision
making have been based around the dominance of the majority and of the superior argument. As a result, decisions are
taken on the basis of the victor's conventional wisdom and
not based on new thinking to meet new challenges. All we
learn, perhaps we have learned it too well, is to be "political"
and get the numbers on our side and to only value debating
skill as a means of sharing ideas.

Perhaps the arts of dialogue and conversation can help us
learn more creatively. For some, of course, these have not
been lost. For many of us, however, this will mean opening
our minds to the new, or to styles of learning and relating
buried deep in our cultural past. In dialogue and conversation
we have an opportunity to put ourselves and our personal pri-
orities aside and together create a collectively held space, a
truly ecumenical space, through which new understanding
can emerge.

This creation of shared meaning through dialogue and
conversation is more than a process of synthesis between
what each of us brings. It means being silent to listen rather
than waiting impatiently for our turn to speak. It means re-
examining the validity of our own assumptions. It means
offering our knowledge and experience rather than imposing
it. It means knowing the starting point but being totally open
to what may emerge. It means taking time. It is the exact

opposite of the precisely framed learning curriculum or the well-prepared business agenda that presupposes most decisions. It is enough to drive a control freak mad! It could be enough to transform our communities and organizations. We have much to learn.

NOTES

[1] H. Gardner, *Intelligence Reframed: Multiple Intelligences for the 21st Century*, New York, Basic Books, 1999, p.60.
[2] Daniel Goleman outlined his concept in his best-selling book *Emotional Intelligence: Why it can matter more than IQ*, New York, Bantam, 1997.
[3] For example, Peter Senge, *The Fifth Discipline: The Art and Practice of the Learning Organization*, New York, Doubleday, 1994.

6. Teaching, Resources and Learning

What was your most recent experience of formal or structured learning? Was it school or college, a training course for your work, Christian education in the local congregation or something like learning to paint pictures?

What use have you made of what you learned? Would it have been better to learn in a different way?

I often think that one of the most helpful things we could do to take learning seriously would be to ban the use of the word "teaching". This might eliminate our preoccupation with it. We learn infinitely more than we are ever taught. The act of teaching does not necessarily imply that any kind of learning actually happens. When I have been a student I have discovered this to my cost and when I have been a teacher I have to confess its reality to my shame.

Teaching is, of course, a useful activity but only as one of the means of supporting learning. My problem with teaching is that it has come to represent a process of transmitting information from the teacher to the student. We looked at the inadequacy of this kind of transmission in Chapter 1. This chapter will focus on formal or structured learning in ecumenical education and it will refer to teaching. Teaching ecumenism, though, is not what ecumenical education is about. Rather, it is about learning to be ecumenical.

The challenge of Paulo Freire

In his last book, translated into English as *Pedagogy of Freedom*, Paulo Freire had much to say about the connection between teaching and learning: "Whoever teaches learns in the act of teaching and whoever learns teaches in the act of learning."[1] Freire wrote that "... to teach is not *to transfer knowledge* but to create possibilities for the production or construction of knowledge". These have been among Freire's constant themes. The teacher is not simply the transmitter of received knowledge and values. Nor is the teacher merely a facilitator of educational processes. The teacher and the student have a common task of producing knowledge. Both bring past knowledge of different kinds, explore what each other knows and what one can teach the other. The result of the dialogue between the teacher as learner and the learner as teacher is social as well as individual change.

One of the areas of education with which Freire was most concerned was that of literacy, both in the basic sense of being able to read and write and in the metaphorical sense of being able to read the world. His methodologies combined the development of the mechanics of reading with critical tools. The result should be an active critical consciousness. Freire embodies the worst nightmares of those in the West who in earlier times resisted giving access to education to the working class for fear they would question the world order or have ideas above their position in life.

I have already observed that there is still a tendency in the churches to resist the development of critical thinking in relation to faith. Ecumenical education is a means of helping us to read the world critically and to act. It is a challenge to churches where education and nurture are processes that domesticate people into a narrow religious status quo because ecumenical education will cause people to question anti-ecumenical or non-ecumenical attitudes and behaviour. Ecumenical education may become uncomfortable to those committed to the ecumenical cause because it encourages critical thinking about the ecumenical movement and its institutions.

For Freire, teaching always involves an ethical approach, for instance in a determination to combat racial, sexual and class discrimination. There must be respect for what students know and for their autonomy and dignity. Teachers as learners are not independent of the social process and require the capacity to be critical. This includes critical reflection on the teacher's own practice. We have to be engaged in uniting theory and practice. Words should be incarnated in example.

Teaching is a human act

Freire reminds us that teaching is a human act. Those of us who work in parts of the world where the humanity of education is in danger of being buried under an avalanche of techniques, technologies and testing need to hear this. There is, of course, nothing wrong with techniques and technologies that aid learning. There is everything wrong with testing where it deliberately excludes the humanity of education and concentrates on facile statistical outcomes. We do seem to be far too impressed with the cleverness of technologies and techniques and let them dictate rather than enable.

Once we have set up institutions in buildings, acquired white boards, overhead projectors, videos and computers and discovered the latest methodological innovations, our idea of what is good and what it possible is controlled by these artifices. In England there is currently a campaign for "real education", by which is meant a return to children sitting silently in neat rows being instructed by a teacher. I want to borrow this title but not its objective. Real education must always centre on the dynamic interaction between teachers and learners as human beings. Our humanity is the principal resource for all education. Ecumenical education should begin with our human selves in our context and use our human interaction as its foundational methodology.

The concept of teaching as a human act points us to the quality and creativity of relationships between teachers and learners. Teachers should know how to listen; silence is as fundamental as speaking. Teaching requires a sense of curiosity, a recognition of our own conditioning and an awareness that we are "unfinished". It is about opening ourselves and taking risks, since the exercise of teaching does not leave us untouched.

Teaching is a process full of joy and hope because it is based on a conviction that change is possible. Freire believed that people are conditioned but not determined by circumstances. Central to the process of education is the learner's critical reflection on the social, economic and cultural conditions in which education happens. He was convinced of the human capacity for greatness rather than mediocrity. We should refuse to live with attitudes of destructive resignation in the face of oppression. Teaching and learning that is carried out with feeling and joy does not preclude serious education.

Freire knew that his rejection of the schooling model of education meant that his understanding and practice of education was not regarded as serious by traditional academics. Of course, it was seen as all too serious in another sense by those who were threatened by the development of people's critical consciousness. I want to claim that ecumenical education, at least potentially, is serious education. For it to be anything other than serious would be to fail the learners and the vision of the ecumenical movement.

While writing this book I had two relevant experiences. One involved listening to a professor of theology telling students that although both theological study and the spirituality and practice of faith were important, the two were separate universes. The formal academic assessment could only take account of the outcomes of study in the lecture room and library. The other experience was a visit to an ecumenical theological education institution where traditional academic study, experience and practice were integrated. The diploma or degree awarded depended not only on an ability to understand the traditional theological disciplines but to demonstrate their connection to context and practice in active ways.

This is Freire on the subject:

Intellectuals who memorize everything, reading for hours on end, slaves to the text, fearful of taking a risk, speaking as if they were reciting from memory, fail to make any concrete connections between what they have read and what is happening in the world, the country or the local community. They repeat what has been read with precision but rarely teach anything of personal value. They speak correctly about dialectical thought but think mechanistically.[2]

Ecumenical education demands the integration of conceptual knowledge, experience and practice. It is, in fact, more demanding and rigorous than traditional academic or schooling approaches. It cannot be done without research or rigour, those shibboleths of traditional academia. For Freire, teaching is about searching, questioning and being submitted to questions. This is serious education because it promotes change in us and in our contexts and communities.

Cooperative learning

One of the features of contemporary educational practices that Freire questioned is the emphasis on individualistic and competitive learning. Throughout society, from commerce to social services, competition is seen as the motivator of efficiency and quality. I would not want to be doctrinaire and insist that there is no place for competition in ecumenical education. However, there is another concept that is more important, both from our Christian roots and from sheer communal pragmatism – cooperation. *Cooperation* is about working together to accomplish shared goals. Within cooperative learning activities we seek outcomes that are beneficial to ourselves and to all other group members. *Cooperative learning* in formal or structured educational contexts uses small groups so that students work together to maximize their own and each other's learning.

Cooperative learning reflects some ideals of community. We benefit from and celebrate the success of each other; we create a common future with our fate lying in each other's hands; we can not do it without one another. No individual, student or teacher possesses all of the information, skills or resources necessary. Freire reminded us that the values of educational methodologies must be consistent with our values. This makes cooperative learning styles particularly appropriate for ecumenical education.

Cooperative learning encourages positive interdependence among students. Competitive learning, on the other hand, requires students to work against each other. In other words, students only achieve success by others failing to do as well as they do – a negative interdependence. The outcomes of co-operative, competitive and individualistic learning have been studied over many years. The indications are that the typical results of cooperative learning are higher achievement, more caring, supportive and committed relationships, and greater social competence. This makes cooperative styles of learning powerful as well as appropriate tools for ecumenical education.

We may be convinced of the desirability of cooperative learning but it will not necessarily happen simply by putting people into groups. It will only happen when we recognize that the contribution of every member of the group is indispensable and that every member has a unique contribution to make from his or her experience, knowledge and skills. This is the sense of positive interdependence that is necessary for the group to be effective. This will be easier to achieve in some situations of ecumenical education than in others. If people are trying to learn how to respond ecumenically to a particular issue in their context, the communal outcome may be of far greater significance than individual performance. Where individuals are taking a course on ecumenism that has been prescribed for them, it may require more work to encourage them to see their success resting in the success of the group. If they do learn that, however, they will have done a significant piece of ecumenical learning.

Part of the solution to the latter kind of problem in formal learning is the development of both individual and group accountability. The group should be accountable for achieving its goals and each member should be accountable for contributing his or her input. Individual accountability includes the appropriateness and style of the contribution in addition to the quality of its content. One of the important things we can learn in a cooperative situation is that it is not sufficient just to have knowledge in our memory. We also have to know how and when to use that knowledge to benefit the work of the group. As well as being a means of communal learning, cooperative learning also develops individual competency.

To be effective, co-operative learning groups need to become places where we teach our knowledge to one another (checking for understanding), talk about concepts being learned and connect past with present learning. They are opportunities for sharing resources and for giving and receiving encouragement. If groups are to be effective we have to develop social skills such as leadership, decision making, trust building, communication and conflict management. In cooperative learning, we have to engage simultaneously in task work (the subject or issue) and in teamwork. It is not an easy or simple option compared to individualistic learning.

Community-based learning

Community-based learning is an established feature of many educational courses. It is known under a variety of names such as field studies, placements or internships. I have just emphasized the importance of basing learning on what we already know. We also need to recognize the importance of offering other experiences from which learning may develop, although we must not ignore the potential of the day-to-day experiences of individuals living in their communities.

We can make some general observations about intentional community-based learning:

It is most effective when there are experiences the student would not otherwise have had. I give two instances as examples – a Baptist ordinand being placed in a Roman Catholic parish, and a student from a comfortable background working in a drop-in centre in an area of social deprivation. The aim is not simply to experience culture shock, although that can stimulate learning.

The greater the exposure, the greater the opportunity for learning. This means that a brief, one-off visit will not be as effective as an involvement over a few weeks or months.

Participating is more effective than observing. Observers need have no commitment other than to their learning objectives. Participants have to be committed to that for which they are working. Having the opportunity to share other people's lives is an immense privilege and a potentially powerful formative experience.

We need to be imaginative in identifying places for community-based learning. The obvious choices of church-related situations are not the only ones. Entirely secular or even other faith-related situations can offer experiences conducive to theological reflection.

An experience will remain no more than an experience unless we deliberately create opportunities to learn from it. This is the most important thing to say about community-based learning. It is possible to have a wonderful experience but to learn nothing from it. It is the responsibility of the teacher to ensure that there are opportunities to learn from experiences.

We have to use two particular skills to learn from our experiences – the ability to accurately describe the experience and critical thinking. At the same time, we have to bring into the dialogue what else we know, particularly in ecumenical education, from the resources of our faith. There is some benefit in making time to do this on one's own. It is much better, however, to do it in a group context where the other members can help us make sense of our experience and to learn how we can make use of it. The same applies to our day-to-day experiences. We need to create frequent opportunities when we can integrate and understand our experiences and other knowledge. We should probably be doing this as part of an ongoing discipline even without the framework of formal study.

The power of story

Bring a group of old friends together and what do they do? Tell stories. Do you remember when this happened to us, when she did this or when he said that? What links us together as people are shared experiences, so we remember them when we meet. We do not usually go in for heavy analysis about what makes us friends or why we want to meet. We tell stories.

Christians are bound together by a story that we tell in reading the Bible and as we respond to Jesus saying, "Do this in remembrance of me" (Luke 22:19).

Although I want to concentrate on face-to-face story-telling, I also observe that sales of novels run high in all languages. Millions watch television soap operas. The predicted demise of cinema and live theatre has not only not happened but the declines in some regions have been reversed. Storytelling groups are being formed in libraries and other public places. Storytelling is offered as a subject by colleges. We can't seem to get enough stories.

We can imagine the importance of stories for early humans gathered around their fires in a world that was dangerous, confusing and unpredictable. This parallels, in fact, the importance of stories for the young child. In the course of history, humans learned how to explain, predict and control. In this brave new world, science displaced the story. Story was relegated to entertainment and the personal sphere of life. Again, we can see a parallel with children. The life-encompassing story time of the nursery school is replaced as the child grows up by separated academic subjects such as maths, science, languages and history.

This displacement of the story is probably more true of the Western world than other regions. In the introduction to *Other Ways of Reading: African Women and the Bible*, Musa W. Dube writes:

> ... stories and story-telling are central to African societies. Stories are told and retold repeatedly to depict life, to transmit values and to give wisdom for survival in life. The art of telling and retelling stories remains central to African societies. For example, a grandmother can tell the same story differently depending on her audience and the issues she wants to address. Thus characters in a story may change to suit the listeners and their circumstances, as the teller sees fit. A story may also be told to a group of listeners who add their comments and questions. This makes story-telling itself (and the story itself) a moment of community writing or interpretation of life, rather than an activity of the teller or author. The teller or writer thus does not own the story or have the last word, but rather the story is never finished: it is a page of the community's fresh and continuous reflection.[3]

Those of us who felt that we had the world under our control have had some unpleasant surprises in recent years. We may have eradicated killer diseases such as smallpox but we are now faced with the new pandemic of HIV/AIDS and the resurgence of old diseases such as malaria. Our industrial production and travel by car and plane have benefited some but brought the effects of global warming on all. The power offered by science to explain, predict and control is not enough. We need to reaffirm or rediscover the different power of story.

The description and analysis of what stories can do fills many books. I will simply list some of these and you can test them out against your own experience. Telling and listening to stories can:

- join people together;
- make connections between generations;
- improve our interpersonal skills;
- help us empathize with others who have different experiences, values and ways of believing;
- enlarge our capacity to feel the full range of emotions;
- exercise our imagination;
- promote creativity;
- develop our capacity for thinking;
- engage us individually and collectively at the same time.

Formal education has encouraged us to develop abstract and analytical forms of discourse. Whereas story-telling comes naturally, we have to learn this language of discourse. We learn to understand by dissecting or breaking down everything into its constituent parts and examining them. Stories, however, allow us to approach and engage life as a whole. We are able to make connections within the story told. Listening also evokes corresponding stories from our experience or context. Stories do not place us in the win/lose situation of traditional discussion. Telling or listening to stories involves us in more of a dance than a fight.

The power of story comes, at least partly, from the direct connection between the words of the story and the person telling it. Print, radio and television can tell stories well and we can interact with the words we hear. What we cannot do through those media is interact with the person speaking. The interaction in face-to-face story-telling can be through the listeners making comments or asking questions, but it may also be subtler through, for instance, body language. Effective story-telling involves the teller reading the listeners and the listeners reading the teller.

The importance of reflection on encounters and experiences has been stressed at several points in this book. Listening to the stories of others can aid reflection. Even more, so can telling our own story. It is often as we articulate events and feelings that we clarify our thinking. I often find that it is in talking about the work of ecumenical education (telling the story) that I gain new insights for myself as well as, hopefully, engaging my listeners. Some people find that keeping a diary that records events and feelings rather than only appointments is a means of reflecting on and making sense of their life. Other people deal with life by writing poems or narratives. Telling our stories is not only about passing on our experiences but about understanding ourselves.

Although we will look at this in more detail in Chapter 8, it is important to mention here the importance of the space we create to tell stories. We need to be comfortable, both physically and mentally. As well as the arrangements of the seating we need to arrange the physical environment to create a good atmosphere. We also have to pay attention to our attitudes and behaviour. If stories are to be told creatively and honestly, a feeling of safety and of mutual trust has to be built up. If you feel that any self-revelation in a story will be used against you, you will not be willing to be open. Discomfort is a distraction.

We can all learn much from indigenous traditions of storytelling that are still practised in many communities. One common feature of several such traditions is the use of a circle. I have discovered from my own experience that two practices, in particular, can be used in ecumenical education. A story expressing the experience or hopes of the group can be built up by one starting and then others continuing the story in turn. The story only emerges through cooperation and it is collectively owned.

The other example is that of the "talking circle", which enables people to tell their stories. Participants pass around an object that has or is given special significance for the group. It is not like the baton in a relay race that is purely practical. The significance of the object, say a stone from the ground or leaves from a tree, should be established at the start. People can only speak when they are holding the object, although they can simply pass it on if they do not want to say anything. The others must listen unconditionally and respectfully. In other words, the listeners cannot control or set limits on what is said. They cannot interrupt to approve, disapprove or correct what is being said. When it is their turn, they must not comment on what others have said but tell their own story.

Telling and listening to stories takes us to the heart of our humanity as individuals and communities. It offers us ways of learning and knowing that are significantly different from those of traditional education.

Learning from what we already know

There are many possible starting points for any learning activity. These may arise from within the reality of a context. They also may be imposed externally by the requirements of a curriculum or validating body for a course. One starting point should be constant, whatever other starting points are also adopted – the knowledge, experience and skills of the learner. We are not blank sheets of paper on which others may write. We each carry with us a rich resource on which any new learning should build.

We are the definitive text on our life. What we may not know is how to read ourselves. Much of the information, concepts, experiences, feelings, attitudes and so on that we carry around with us are unconsidered. To learn from our own learning we need not only opportunities to pour this out, we also need space for reflection. I always try to begin work-shops, consultations and seminars for which I am responsible with opportunities for participants to begin to contribute from their own experience and knowledge. At the very least, it stops me from wasting time by telling them what they already know! I believe it also does three important things – it enables participants to make sense of their own learning in dialogue with others who are trying to do the same thing; it gives a clear message that we are all contributors to the learning process; it means that subsequent learning will be rooted in the contexts to which participants return.

Taking people's existing learning seriously does not mean taking it at face value. Having respect for and using what people already know does not mean letting everything go unquestioned or unexamined. We learn to read ourselves by being questioned and challenged. In this process we can develop our own critical consciousness of our knowledge and ourselves. Otherwise education would be a matter of reinforcing our existing prejudices and partial understandings. A starting point is exactly what is says it is, the place from which we move.

One of the problems of formal education that is imposed on children or adults is that the learning that happens is likely to be compartmentalized. For ecumenical education not to take the person as one of its starting points would be to act in an inconsistent manner. By its nature, ecumenical education, like all theological education, should be integrative. We are whole people living in community. We must ensure that our experience in our denomination is related to our ecumenical experience. What we read in denominational texts must be engaged with what we read in ecumenical texts. The experience of life inside the local congregation has to be related to our experience in our local and global communities. We should begin with where we are and not try to construct an ecumenical learning experience that treats our past as a closed book.

I am not at all surprised that many courses in ecumenism do not result in ecumenically minded and active people. If we begin, as many courses do, with the history of the ecumenical movement or by reading ecumenical texts rather than by engaging the student's own ecumenical knowledge and experience, we must expect only the kind of knowledge that is good for getting qualifications but makes no positive impact on us.

Using other resources for learning

There are three kinds of learning resources for ecumenical education – our own lives in their context, people who can help us reflect and who are themselves learners, and the products of other people's historical and contemporary learning. That the first two are people is immensely significant.

The third kind of learning resource, of course, is not insignificant. Yet because ecumenical education is about transformation rather than transmission, it cannot be pre-eminent. This third category brings together what we might call knowledge, data, information, theories, concepts, traditions and wisdom. It is stored in all kinds of ways—on the printed page, the hard disk of a computer, on audiotape or videotape and in our memories. The ecumenical movement has itself produced a large volume of printed paper and knowledge recorded in other ways.

The Internet

A recent debate at the Royal Institution in London on the influence of the Internet, which took place in front of a high-level academic audience, raised some interesting issues about our engagement with such knowledge. On the positive side, participants said that the Internet's potential to make information instantly available to millions of people at marginal cost was as radical a development as the invention of the printing press in the 15th century or even the emergence of language. On the negative side, participants argued that the vast array of unregulated information on the Internet would undermine education. When so much information is available at the touch of a button, we will no longer need to gain knowledge in the traditional sense by storing information in our own memories. The primary issue for education has been putting knowledge into students' heads but now it will have to be showing them how to navigate in that electronic world. Some raised the vision of human teachers being sidelined. When human beings are no longer needed to control the technological structure, some raised a question about the place for emotions such as love and compassion and for other uniquely human things in the learning process.

What surprised me in reading the account of this debate was the argument that education was seen as storing information in people's memories. Now it would be foolish to pretend that we do not need to carry a certain amount of information around in our heads for the purposes of daily living. I need the information stored in my head about how to work the computer I am using to write this. I cannot read the instruction manual (even if I could understand it!) each time I want to access a file or save a document. We need to learn, formally or informally, all kind of things to live our lives and do our work. That said, the days are long gone when an "educated" person could carry around in his or her memory the sum of human knowledge. The exponential growth of human knowledge means that even libraries full of books cannot contain it all in an accessible form.

Even when it was possible to know most of what there was to know, I hope education was also about critical thinking – knowing how to assess and make use of knowledge. This is what we most need to learn. The Internet with its seemingly infinite store of knowledge of infinitely variable quality makes this kind of education imperative. It is often said that the quality of our decision making depends both on the quality of the decision-making process and the quality of the information on which the decision is based. We need to develop skills in both assessing the appropriateness and reliability of what we find on Web pages and being able to use the information and understanding we acquire for the common good.

If the advent of the Internet challenges the simplistic transmission model of education, we should rejoice. Feats of memory may be impressive and win prizes on television quiz shows but in formal education and in real life there should be no marks for just reproducing information. The effective person is the one who knows what value to put on information and how to use it, whose mind is equipped with evaluative, categorization and concept-making skills. Christians should know this: "Not everyone who says to me, 'Lord, Lord' [i.e. the right words] will enter the kingdom of heaven, but only the one who does the will of the Father [i.e. attitudes, relationships and actions]" (Matt. 7:21).

In the counter-argument to the value of the Internet, teachers were seen to have the task of manipulating and regulating knowledge. Thus they would be put out of business by the more efficient mechanism of the Internet. Rather than make the case myself, I return to Paulo Freire, who sees the interaction between the teacher as learner and the learner as teacher as a human process involving the affective as well as the cognitive. Teaching is not about manipulating knowledge so that the correct message is received. The essentially and uniquely human things, such as our emotions, are precisely the reason we need teachers. To reduce education to people picking up whatever knowledge they can from the Internet or even from books would be to dehumanize us.

Sometimes I think that educators in the North have an infatuation with information/communication/education technology. Infatuation is always a dangerous state of being because it blinds us to reality. Our quality of education appears to be validated by our ability to have PowerPoint presentations, show videos and have interactive teaching tools on computers. Such things are useful but they are neither the foundational nor the most powerful agents of learning. That always was and still is human interaction in community. The point of a classroom (or a church, for that matter) is that it is a place of community where we can learn together. All the technology, including the Internet, only makes sense as an adjunct to the personal and community processes and not as a substitute.

Human authority of all kinds, including in the churches, has a bad track record of denying people access to knowledge. Centuries ago there were those who argued against teaching everyone to read. If people could read things for themselves, they said, there would be no need for authority figures to tell them what they needed to know and think. Certainly there was and still are plenty of dubious or downright evil things in books. Many centuries ago, the Geek philosopher Socrates thought it was dangerous for people to learn by reading but for a very different reason. He believed that the interaction between people in asking and answering questions developed critical thinking. The challenge of learning how to understand and apply knowledge is the same for the printed page as for the electronic page. The freedom to access and read books does not do teachers out of a job, nor should the Internet. The ability to freely access and be able to make use of information should be a democratic right. Our concern should be that everyone has that opportunity.

This question of access to the learning resources of knowledge is important. I have visited, for instance, theological colleges and seminaries in some parts of the world where their whole library contains significantly fewer books than can be found on my own bookshelves. Building up libraries, resource banks of audiotapes and videotapes and providing Internet access in the congregation and beyond is vital. Where Internet access is possible, it provides access to a vast amount of written material and images from the ecumenical movement. Both courses and resources are available online.

Books, Internet access and everything else do little on their own. As I have said, we all need to learn how to read these resources critically. Unfortunately, some education in the churches encourages people to read some things uncritically and to dismiss others out of hand. The critical reading of the text on a printed page, on a screen or of our lives is a basic task of ecumenical education.

Although it is now no longer possible for anyone to know everything, we all need to know how to find out anything. We already know this in connection with daily living. We know how to use the Yellow Pages telephone directory to find someone to do something for us or we know the right person to ask for that information. We are, in fact, all used to finding out things. We all use basic research strategies but it is only when I describe them as such that they seem anything out of the ordinary.

In ecumenical education, we often lack a basic under-standing of what exists in the way of knowledge that has been produced in and through the ecumenical movement. Some may be aware of significant ecumenical studies such as the WCC paper *Baptism, Eucharist and Ministry* and use the various books that have come from that as resources for their own local learning processes. Fewer will be aware of the vast array of ecumenical reports and other documentation on racism, the environment, disability, human rights, peace building and so on that could be useful for their contextual reflection on these issues. We do not only need to learn how to look, but also where to look for appropriate learning resources.

What makes ecumenical education ecumenical is not its content or subject matter. I make no apology for the fact that you will not find in this book a list of ecumenical set texts that everyone should read or those particular aspects of ecu-menical history that everyone should know. The goal is trans-formation and the content is determined by the people and the context. The resources that drive ecumenical education are human resources. It is obviously easier for me coming from a knowledge resource rich environment to place the emphasis on human resources. Having said that, we ignore the primacy of human resources at our peril.

Ways of learning together

I want to point to three ways of supporting learning in for-mal ecumenical educational settings that do not involve standing at the front of a class telling students what they should know. These are only examples and I would encour-age you to develop your own approaches that suit your ways of working and are appropriate to your situation. There is no question that these methods are more demanding than giving a lecture. It is no accident that these come after my reflections on Freire, co-operative learning and the use of experience. They should be read and assessed in the light of all of that.

Enquiry teaching is a process that involves students rais-ing and answering questions relating to contemporary and historical ecumenical issues. It can be applied to something as general as the development of the ecumenical movement or as specific as appropriate intervention in conflict situations. There are various forms of enquiry teaching but the basic structure can be represented by six stages:

1. identifying the issues and problems within a given area – generating appropriate questions;
2. proposing a hypothesis – identifying the possible explanations or solutions and developing a hypothesis to be tested;
3. researching – collecting and organizing evidence. This stage is more difficult than it looks. Students will have to understand the difference between primary and secondary sources, recognize relevant data and categorize it;
4. evaluating, analyzing and interpreting the evidence – testing the hypothesis;
5. concluding – drawing inferences from the proving or disproving of the hypothesis;
6. reporting – presenting the outcomes.

It is worth considering what the process of enquiry teaching involves. Students generate their own knowledge co-operatively rather than receiving it. They are consequently more likely to know how to use it. The process encourages divergent and creative thinking. It involves critical thinking in terms of analysis, synthesis and evaluation. The requirement to present the outcome of the process encourages clarity of thinking.

Problem-solving is not only a useful skill to learn, it can also be a means of learning. It can be a good exercise to apply to the issues that arise from the daily experience of students or from community learning experiences. In many ways it is similar to enquiry teaching. Many writers have systematized an exemplary problem-solving process. The following is a summary of the basic aspects found in most descriptions:

1. identify and define the problem;
2. describe and represent the problem;
3. consider what knowledge, skills and resources are needed;
4. identify possible strategies and decide a plan;

5. act;
6. evaluate;
7. consider the wider implications for future activity.

Sometimes it may be necessary to break down complex problems into smaller constituent problems and to work through each. If ecumenical education is to be integrating, an important aspect of problem solving should be to bring to bear what has been learned elsewhere.

Reciprocal teaching is particularly appropriate for engaging with ecumenical texts such as *Baptism, Eucharist and Ministry* or the reports of bilateral church dialogues. It gives a structure for helping students relate to and understand what they read. It consists of four stages:

1. Summarizing – students identify what they consider to be the most significant information in the text and summarize it in their own words. Depending on the context and the capabilities and experience of the students, this might be larger or smaller sections of the text.
2. Generating questions – students ask questions about the material and see whether there are answers in the text
3. Clarifying – students consider where and why the text may be difficult to understand. They may identify problems with vocabulary or with not having sufficient background knowledge. Both the students and the teacher will work to answer one another's questions. This may require research outside the formal session.
4. Predicting – students are asked to consider what ought to come next beyond their current reading. In doing this they should not only draw on what they have engaged with already but on their existing knowledge and experience. The latter is to encourage them to see how the text relates to their own contexts.

The sequence then repeats itself with the next section of text. This process of active engagement with the text has the potential to create a depth of understanding unlikely to be achieved by a discourse on the text from the teacher. It is also a process that students can subsequently use with groups outside formal educational structures.

Reforming the formal

The problem of formal education is not that it organizes learning. As we have observed, even informal learning needs a pattern or process that involves both experience and reflection for it to be effective. The problem of formal education is that the form controls the learning rather than the learning being facilitated by the form. There are many courses in ecumenism in well-respected institutions that I could not describe as ecumenical education. They transmit a certain amount of knowledge of the history, theology and activities of the ecumenical movement but in a dispassionate manner. Students may learn about ecumenism but do not develop ecumenical attitudes. That kind of thing is not, the validating institutions say, an academic task. There is confusion between traditional academic practice and the quality of learning – failure, if you like, to apply the much-valued intellectual rigour to their own processes.

A true ecumenical education cannot be under subjugation to an external institution if it is to be contextual and creative. That does not mean that its quality cannot be validated for certificates, diplomas and degrees, where that is appropriate. There is an increasing number of examples of creative thinking in course design that brings together experience and traditional forms of knowledge. Such courses assess, not the students' ability to understand received knowledge in a kind of academic vacuum, but the quality of thought in their engagement.

Sometimes formal ecumenical education will have to critically reflect on its own form and thus transform its educational environment.

NOTES

[1] Paulo Freire, *Pedagogy of Freedom*, Lanham, MD, Rowman & Littlefield, 1998, pp. 30f.
[2] *Ibid.* p. 34
[3] M.W. Dube ed., *Other Ways of Reading: African Women and the Bible*, Atlanta/Geneva, Society of Biblical Literature/WCC, 2001, p. 3.

7. Spectators or Participants?

> Think back over the past week and identify three occasions when you felt as though you were a spectator observing what was happening around you.
>
> Also identify three occasions when you felt really involved with what was going on.
>
> These can be from any part of your life – home, work, church or leisure.
>
> For you, what is the difference between being a spectator and being a participant?

"Participation is good, participation is right, participation is necessary." While this is not a quotation, it could well be. It sounds like the kind of doctrinaire slogan from a totalitarian regime that George Orwell satirized in his book *Animal Farm*. If we say it enough times, we will believe it. There is a sense in which we have and we do. I will confess that sometimes during seminars and workshops I inwardly groan when I am expected to be involved in this exercise or that. It would be easier and more comfortable just to sit back and listen and watch. Anyway, I am not always convinced that all such exercises really have an educational purpose. Could it be that they are provided merely to give an impression of participation?

To help us think through the importance of participation we will begin by considering three small scenes that I hope will be recognizable even if not familiar.

Scene 1. The speaker comes to the end of the lecture and sits down to polite applause. The moderator of the meeting stands and says, "We have about ten minutes before we need to finish. Are there any questions?" Members of the audience raise some points and the speaker replies. In closing the meeting, the moderator comments, "I am glad we were able to make it a participative exercise."

Who is participating here? We might say that it was only the speaker, the moderator and the particular members of the audience who asked questions. That would be equating participation with a particular kind of activity, speaking. What about everyone else? Does being physically present mean participation? or being present and taking notes on what is said? or being present and engaging conceptually with the lecture? All of these involve different kinds of activity. It is possible to be present in the room, yet somewhere else far distant in one's thoughts. We can write down very full notes on what is being said without it having any kind of impact on us. We can be intellectually stimulated, yet learn nothing. We can come away with more information than when we arrived but still think and behave in exactly the same manner; in other words, the exercise has made no difference to us.

We may wonder why the moderator found it necessary to remark on the lecture becoming a participatory exercise. Perhaps, overwhelmed by the educational dogma "participation is good, participation is right, participation is necessary", the occasion had to be legitimized by its being labelled participative.

Scene 2. The children in the classroom are busy in small groups preparing to present the project they have been researching over the past few days. One group is writing information sheets, one preparing a dramatic presentation, another creating a visual display. The teacher is, in turn, resource-supplier, encourager and order-keeper. A visiting adult is overheard saying, "We didn't have all this participation in my day. We had to sit at our desks and be taught."

The children could be described as participating in learning but within certain limits. The teacher was not only there to enable but also to maintain the boundaries. Some limitations may be necessary for safety and good order. However, the temptation is always for these boundaries to be for the convenience of the teacher or the educational institution. Although this kind of learning may often lead to the teacher learning something new from the children's research, the desired outcome of the exercise is already defined by a required curriculum or by the teacher's own lesson plan.

It is a form of subversion of Paulo Freire's educational ideals. The teacher as the one who teaches what he or she knows to those who do not know is replaced by the teacher who sets up a learning experience so that what he or she knows is learned by those who do not know. Given that there is no necessary connection between the act of teaching and the act of learning, the latter may be judged essentially better than the former. However, that is as far as it goes. A form of participation is used (or abused) as a means to a predetermined end.

The remark of the visitor is another reaction to "participation is good, participation is right, participation is necessary". Far from having been brainwashed into acceptance, the whole notion of participation has probably been dismissed as modish and trendy as compared with the solid virtue of "traditional" teaching methods.

Scene 3. As the hours went by, you could notice the difference as children, women and men worked hard to clean up their neighbourhood. The community clean-up day did not just involve physical activity; there was a street fair on environmental issues with a puppet show and story-telling circle. At the end of the day, the whole community gathered together to celebrate.

Perhaps no one ever used the words participation or learning during any of the activities. Identifying participative learning may be useful but it is implementing it that is vital. In many ways this scene sounds ideal – young and old involved together. However, participation in activity may not be participation in learning. Doing can be an unreflective activity. The end result of a clean community environment is an important outcome. For that environment to remain clean there has to be learning that leads on to further action and an understanding of the wider issues that affect the community from outside. The street fair may be an attempt to do this but unless people are given opportunity and encouragement to identify and reflect on the experience of their activity, learning may not happen. We also should note that this was a special exercise which, although it was in everyday life, does not necessarily relate to learning through everyday life.

This scene also touches on another important issue. In the other two scenes, learning, although it was done in a communal setting, was an individual activity. Here, there is the possibility of community learning. This means collective learning as community in distinction to the total of individual learning of all those who make up the community.

Participative learning

Unless you have specific learning difficulties, learning to speak a language is easy, if you begin at birth. You come into the world and live surrounded by language – spoken, written and in environmental print. You participate in a widening community of relationships as you grow up. This means that you learn your mother tongue without thinking about it. School may help you refine and develop your language skills but only on the basis of what you have learned in other ways. You can even acquire more than one language at once. Studies of children growing up from an early age in bilingual situations show that, far from being confused by two different languages, they respond to the context in the language they use and are not impaired in their intellectual development. We cannot remember learning to speak our language. That is how easy it was.

Learning another language later on in life is not at all easy. It is not only knowing the vocabulary, it is also learning the subtle patterning of the words in their correct form that makes communication possible. You have to work at it. A few words strung haphazardly together may enable you to buy a loaf of bread but will not go far in developing a relationship or exploring ideas.

Two of my friends live in France, a mother and 10-year-old daughter. The daughter was born into an English-speaking home in a French-speaking environment. The mother arrived from England not long before the daughter was born so both have had the same exposure to French. The daughter slips easily between the two languages depending on to whom she is talking. The kind of mistakes she makes in the use of language are those that could be expected at her stage of development. She takes great delight, sometimes with the despair in her voice that only children can have of a parent, in correcting her mother's occasional failure to use French in quite the right way. Even being immersed in another language for a period of time does not remove the requirement of some effort to be in complete control of it.

Why is there a difference between mother and daughter after an equal amount of time in a French-speaking environment? I suggest that the answer lies, partly at least, in the way in which they have each participated in a natural or informal learning experience. The child is an uninhibited learner, open to experience. The adult is inhibited partly through already being proficient in another language and partly because adults are rarely free spirits in learning. It is not about the duration of participation but the depth – the quality, not the quantity.

Both the child and the mother benefit from opportunities of doing some conscious learning, where what is learned is made explicit: pronunciation, spelling, rules of grammar. Learning done by living in context usually needs to be put in some kind of order, to be codified. My own experience of learning a foreign language was exactly the opposite way around. We sat in a classroom and learned the rules of grammar. We learned the meaning of words, how verbs declined in different tenses and so on. It was hoped that it would all make sense once we encountered the language in real use. It didn't! An experience has to happen first and then the learning to make sense of it and make use of it.

You may wonder why I have spent so much time using the illustration of language learning. I think it is one of the most accessible analogies for religious learning, including ecumenical learning. Language is not just a medium by which we communicate; it influences, if not controls, the structures of our thinking. Ecumenical education helps us learn another kind of knowledge and discourse.

Where do we learn our language as religious people, the words that represent important concepts or doctrines? One kind of answer to that question would talk about Sunday schools, preparation for confirmation/church membership, Bible study groups, training for the ministries of the church and other intentional teaching and learning processes. That answer would not be wrong, but to talk only in those terms would be to miss the most powerful agent that shapes faith and the way we understand it. It is, of course, simply participating in the life of a faith community that develops both our faith and our religious language.

The role of worship

I suggest that it is most particularly through participating in worship that we develop our religious language and thought. Without going in to too much detail, let us look at what is happening in worship. At its best, worship involves the whole of us—body, mind and spirit. All of our physical senses can be involved as well as feelings, imagination and thought. This opens us up, often without our being aware of what is happening, to the words, actions and symbols used in worship.

I am going to reveal my prejudices by saying that I react strongly against those who describe the sermon or homily as an opportunity for teaching. This is especially the case when they proceed to lecture the congregation on what they should believe or do. For me, preaching is more about proclaiming than teaching. Even if you see the sermon as teaching, however, the rest of worship influences learning significantly more. Because of our total involvement and because they are regularly repeated, the words, actions and symbols become part of us. Our theology is likely to be influenced far more by the words of the hymns we sing than the books we read. Because this kind of learning through participation is subtle, we do not recognize that it happens.

In general terms, this reminds us that it is not only through a sense of liturgical correctness that we should pay attention to the words, actions and symbols of our worship. Words, actions and symbols that do not possess a Christian integrity have a consequent outcome in what participants in worship actually learn. This is unsatisfactory from a denominational perspective, let alone a wider one.

More specifically for ecumenical education, we have to be aware of what can be a powerful vaccination against the development of an ecumenical attitude or discourse. Although many constituents of worship are common Christian property – for example, scripture, many liturgical elements, some prayers and hymns – it does not always feel like that. As I have remarked elsewhere, we have an unfortunate propensity for asserting, if only by implication rather than direct statement, ownership by the denomination or even local congregation. This makes it difficult for people to feel their relatedness and commonality across the church. Worship that is done in a denominational context and according to denominational norms can influence an openness of attitude, but only if we have that intention.

Informal learning

We learn, then, far more than we are ever taught. Most of what we learn throughout our lives is acquired in an informal manner or incidentally to other activities. Some of the most fundamental things come without sitting in a classroom or taking a course. All people develop a set of values by which they live. Observers may think that the values of some people are false, inconsistent or downright evil. Nevertheless, our values determine our behaviour and attitudes. In spite of the calls of those who demand that people should be taught "right and wrong" through formal educational processes in schools and religious communities, it seems to be powerfully the case that values are acquired informally through participating in communities that are significant to the person. The primary location of values development is the home. As children grow into adulthood, other influences on values are peer groups and religious communities. However, the influence comes not from the stated values of families or churches, but from those actually practised. I have remarked earlier on the ability of children to spot inconsistencies between our ideals and what we do, and our seeming inability to change our individual and communal lives so that our learning is positive.

We may think informal learning that takes place through the business of living is easy because we do not notice it happening, even though the processes of learning in our brains is complex. The more formal learning is, the more we notice that we are in the process of learning. When I began writing this book, I intended to devote a great deal of attention to informal learning as opposed to the rather overvalued formal learning. As I reflected on what I have been writing, I came to a rather different conclusion.

We need to recognize the value of both informal and formal learning and redress the balance of esteem between the two. Perhaps all good learning needs to involve both. What is most important, however, is the quality of participation in both. As we have seen, it is possible to have a powerful experience and still learn nothing because we have not participated in a learning process. We can sit in the lecture or seminar but not participate in learning. The quality and effectiveness of learning is usually related to the degree to which the learner is an active participant.

Participatory learning and participation

There can be a significant difference between participatory approaches to learning and real participation. Participatory activities provide opportunities for people to be more engaged in the learning process than traditional teaching methods, which tend to be passive approaches. They include activities such as group discussion, role-play or simulation. Even when group discussion takes place in a context related to the learning, it is possible to exchange ideas and information only at the level of theory. Even worse, there can be a tendency for discussion to become competitive with participants trying to "score points" off one another or to defend a position at any cost.

Many of us have had experiences where group discussion is not an open learning but the conflict of closed minds. Role-play gives us the opportunity to become someone else in a given situation and explore the options of attitudes and behaviour. Simulations allow us to explore what it means to be ourselves in a given situation. These two approaches have their strengths and are particularly appropriate where it could be destructive to explore attitudes and behaviour in real life. But in all participatory learning activities there is an element of artificiality or distance from the area of learning. Participation, on the other hand, is a direct involvement in that part of life where learning is taking place.

Awareness-raising, which has sometimes been seen as the objective of ecumenical education, is no longer enough. Among churches where traditional denominational boundaries are still being reinforced, raising awareness of the ecumenical vision and possibilities might be considered an advance. However, ecumenical education should result in people living with ecumenical attitudes and putting ecumenism into practice. This has implications for the style and depth of participation.

We can see a progression in the need for participatory approaches to actual participation:

Participatory approaches as a means of raising awareness; moving to Participatory approaches as a means of encouraging/enabling participation; moving to Participation in a particular action or in everyday life as a learning experience.

As I have said, participatory approaches may have an element of artificiality about them. Simulations, games and case studies, for example, may contain elements of real life but they are undertaken in a safe and bounded environment. Participation in life itself is neither safe nor bounded. It is potentially the most significant learning opportunity we have, but we have to learn how to use it creatively. In other words, approaches to participatory learning should result in participation. In the end, participation itself is the primary learning experience.

I expect that most of us at some time or other have been attracted by that strand that runs through most religions of withdrawal from the world. The world is a messy, untidy and unpleasant place where we may get dirty or even injured. It is much safer to withdraw into a community of like-minded people who think, believe and act as we do. Where can we learn most about God and the challenge that knowledge gives for being and acting? We are unlikely to learn much if we only interact with those who know what we know and think what we think. Our participation in everyday life is where we can both learn and act out the implication of a God who loves us. The raw material of learning and action is life itself in all its complexity. In taking the learner as the starting point for learning in ecumenical education, I do not just mean the individual but the communal context in which the individual lives.

This means that in ecumenical education we should be looking to the primary experiences of encounter and involvement with the other – other people, other cultures, other situations – as the basis for our learning.

Taking responsibility for learning

When play in a football match flows and is not constantly disrupted by free kicks for infringements, the referee is often complimented on a sensible use of the whistle. Perhaps the players should also be complimented on taking responsibility for keeping play within the laws of the game. The very presence of a referee, however, means that most players will let him or her take responsibility for maintaining the laws of the game and will try to see what they can get away with without being penalized.

Teachers, tutors, mentors and enablers can have the same kind of effect in the learning situation. Even if they do not overtly take control of learning, the learner will tend to hand responsibility over to them as the "experts" (see Chapter 6). There can be no full participation if the learner does not take responsibility for her or his own learning. In fact, it can never be "her or his own learning" if it is under the control of someone else. We all spend much of our lives in school, higher education and the church doing someone else's learning. We end up with someone else's knowledge and even someone else's faith rather than our own. This creates problems for us in living lives that are internally integrated and integrated with the reality of the world we experience.

It may be good for the personal feelings of the teacher in the school or the minister in the congregation to know that they control the learning of others, but it makes for an unhealthy kind of dependency for society or the church. Where people are not encouraged to take responsibility for their own learning, it will not be surprising, for example, that there is no interest in the development of spirituality and active discipleship beyond the formal processes of Christian nurture. Participation implies responsibility.

Participation in reflection

Being active is not enough. It is possible to participate and learn nothing. There needs to be something that enables us to learn from experience. We can label this process reflection, which we discuss elsewhere. Here we need to recognize that there must be an active participation in the self, group or communal process of reflection. We should never accept second-hand interpretations of our own experience. Yet churches are often the worse offenders in telling people what their experience means or how it should be categorized.

Reflection does not only mean sitting and thinking on our own or engaging in dialogue with others. I often find that walking around helps me think. Drawing or singing also can help us reflect. Many people find it useful to do meditative physical exercises such as shibashi. A recent experience in a study group where we did shibashi together every morning reminded me of the difference this can make to our reflective processes.

Many years ago, I was the co-leader of a reflective weekend for a congregation. One of the exercises we did was to use modelling clay to express our faith. It was the children who showed the way by being unafraid of picking up and moulding the modelling clay. The adults were gradually drawn in. Afterwards several of them spoke of that as the most significant part of the weekend. Thinking with their fingers moved them out of their familiar mental tracks.

For effective learning there must be both life participation and reflective participation. This immediately raises the question of ability to participate in both aspects. A full analysis of factors that prevent participation is beyond the scope of this book, but we must at least record some of them: economic means, gender, age, race, location, physical, language, mobility, political, family. All of these in some way or another may make learning through participation difficult, if not impossible. We may have the most participatory processes and we may enable people to learn through participation, but all of that is meaningless unless people are able to participate.

Participation involves the community and the individual

If we understand people in terms of beings in relationship rather than as solitary individuals, the dimension of community has to be part of our understanding of learning. This has two implications. First, the community of which an individual learner is a member must participate in any learning process. We recognize this, for example, in the fact that society establishes state school systems to provide education. However, this usually puts an education system between the community and its schools. Locating learning in the community is a much bigger issue than where schools or courses are placed. Language such as "serving the community" does not take us far enough either. It must go down into rooting learning in the community – spatially, psychologically, relationally, taking into account strengths, weakness, resources and opportunities – so that the community is an active participant.

The second implication is that any community has to learn as community, to be a participant in its own learning. A community does not become a community without a communal learning process. If it does not go on learning to respond and adapt to changing external and internal realities, it will not live on beyond the present. It is much easier to engage individuals within a community than it is to engage the community as a whole. Take the example of what is called institutional racism. Even if all the people who compose the institution do not personally behave in a racist manner, it is still possible for the institutional behaviour to be racist. Communal behaviour is not the sum of the behaviour of all the individuals that make it up. Enabling a community or organization to learn is much more difficult than dealing with the individual learning needs person by person.

Western culture has placed an emphasis on the individual with the result that those of us who have grown up within it find it very difficult to conceive of learning in anything but individual terms. To take a particular example, we have understood Christian nurture to be a process of development of the individual in understanding and living the faith. Consequently we have failed to address the learning needs of the congregation as a communal entity. We have presumed that by enabling individuals to learn, we have enabled the Christian community to learn.

There can be no spectators in ecumenical education. Observation may help us learn about some things. Participation enables learning that transforms.

8. Rearranging the Chairs and Ourselves

> Where do you feel most comfortable – talking to your friends? reading a book? writing a letter?
>
> Is it the same place each time or are some places better for one thing but not the other?
>
> Think about some of the things you do during the week and the place or space in which you do them. What makes a place or a space appropriate for a particular activity?

A local church had to close its sanctuary for a few months so that some essential repairs could be undertaken. Next to the sanctuary there was a church hall used for children's and youth activities, so the congregation transferred its Sunday worship to this hall. They tried various ways of arranging the chairs and in the end discovered that a circular pattern was best. I occasionally preached at that church and after leading worship in the round in their church hall, I asked some members of the congregation about their feelings. Almost universally they said how good it was to be able to see other people's faces when they worshiped rather than the back of their heads.

They felt worship had improved. The preachers were the same people as before, with the same strengths and weaknesses in enabling worship. The hall had no aesthetic qualities to improve the atmosphere. A better experience of community, they said, was created by the different way of arranging the chairs.

Some time after the completion of the work on the sanctuary, I went back to the church to lead worship. Everything was looking good. They had replaced their fixed seating with individual chairs. However, they had arranged them in rows facing the front. They were looking at the back of one another's heads again!

Now they had the opportunity, why did they not experiment with finding good ways to arrange the seats as they had done in the church hall? After all, they had had such a positive experience that almost all affirmed. The first thing to say is that this is yet another illustration of the way that experience, even very positive experience, teaches us nothing unless we reflect on it and make our learning explicit. The second thing, which is the point I want to make here, is that we seem to have in our minds the "right way" of doing things.

In the sanctuary, the right way of arranging the seating was in rows facing the front. That is the way we do things here. Experimentation and change was possible in the hall because it was not the sanctuary. The "right way" of doing things is remarkably persistent even in the face of evidence that there may be better ways.

Those of us who have spent the whole of our formal education from primary school to university sitting in rows facing the front have a tendency to reproduce this for every learning opportunity. This is how real education happens. Anything that does not involve regimented seating cannot be taken seriously. Or so something inside us says.

Rearranging the chairs and tables has never been in my job description but I seem to have spent much time doing it. I regard it as a vital part of the preparation for any meeting, seminar or workshop. So why is the arrangement of the chairs so important?

Where we sit makes a difference

I want to illustrate how the arrangement of seating profoundly affects behaviour and the quality of an experience by taking three examples. They are deliberately not drawn from education, where experiences are not open to general scrutiny. Instead, I have drawn them from the public realm where the effects are more widely observable and documented.

The English are proud to own the "mother of parliaments", the House of Commons in London. The chamber is rectangular in shape with parallel rows of seats facing each other across a long central aisle. What does this imply? Politics is confrontational. There are only two sides, even if there are many political parties. One side is right, the other is wrong. It is good for trading insults and simplistic knock down arguments. But reflective debate that works for better understanding of issues and appropriate legislation to meet needs finds it difficult to flourish. The chamber itself predetermines the style of political interaction within it. Interestingly enough, town halls in England generally have council chambers that are arranged in a semicircular pattern. Perhaps it was thought important to work in a different style locally.

One of my favourite theatres is seven sided. It has three levels of seating that go all the way around. Whereas in a traditional theatre everyone sits facing the stage at the front, there the audience surrounds the actors. In the one the actors play their parts in front of the scenery, in the other they act among the scenery, which is more evocative than realistic. It means that, just as in real life, you see characters front, back and side on. It requires much more imagination on the part of the director and actors and of the audience. It has the capacity to help the audience feel part of the action rather than being only spectators of a drama played out in front of them. The arrangement of the seats creates an entirely different experience of familiar plays.

Of course, sitting around the action is nothing new for sports fans. In football in England, something interesting, though, is happening when new stadiums are being built. The traditional football ground was rectangular in shape with the stands along the sides and ends of the pitch. In many parts of a ground it could be difficult to see the whole pitch, particularly from the corners. At least one or two of these stands would be occupied by fans who felt very territorial about their space. They would chant aggressively and sometimes resort to violent confrontations to protect their territory or even to invade the stand occupied by supporters of the other team. Recently built stadiums have been oval in shape with clear sight lines for all spectators and no structural division of territory. Studies have shown that these more unifying and less confrontational architectural designs have had a significant effect in improving crowd behaviour.

Whether we customarily arrange the seats in our activities out of a feeling of propriety or leave them anyhow because it is only the content that counts, we need to be convinced it matters. I have chosen these examples because they make the point that the arrangement of the seats really does have an effect.

Sitting around

The arrangement of seats can be about control. With everyone sitting in rows facing the teacher, there can be no doubt who controls the learning and the style in which it is done. This formation says that there is one person who has the knowledge, one person who is of interest and value, and that is the one at the front. They will deliver what they think suitable in a style they think appropriate to those sitting in front of them. It may be very interesting or even entertaining, but it is all about the person at the front. The audience is expected to be passive receivers of what is given. No interaction between them is expected. Listeners may ask questions that will be answered authoritatively from the front. Even if someone puts forward a telling argument against the teacher, the very arrangement of the room will favour the authority of the teacher. Having a panel of people instead of an individual does not essentially change things.

A circle is a more democratic shape. It says that there is an equality of position and of the opportunity to give and receive. Participants are able to see one another and speak directly to one another's concerns and issues. People are not only able to hear what is spoken but also to read the body language that accompanies it. Although there may be one or more people with responsibility for the group, they are identified with it rather than placed over against it. Even when substantive inputs are given, they come from within. The shape speaks of a community of learning.

Two events occurred in Harare, Zimbabwe, in December 1998 that show an interesting contrast in seating styles. The first was the festival to mark the conclusion of the Decade of Churches in Solidarity with Women. For the plenary sessions, the seats were arranged around tables. When you entered the plenary hall, it was like coming into an enormous restaurant with all the tables dotted around. Just as in a restaurant, the eight people around each table were able to engage in conversations and to share their experiences and feelings in depth. It was a small thing for some to have to move their chairs to look to the front of the hall when necessary. The eighth assembly of the WCC that followed was set up in a traditional style with rows facing the front. The limitation on discussion and engagement between representatives on the floor of the plenary was very apparent to those who participated in both events. Since then, the work of the WCC's Central Committee has benefited from seating the members around tables.

I have already confessed to preferring the circular style to rows facing the front. I would be less than honest, though, if I did not admit that individuals – official leaders and those self-appointed – can dominate and control what happens in the circle. But I believe that a circle has a greater potential to enable creative ecumenical education.

Comfortable space

There are two more things to be said about furniture before we turn to other ways of opening up the right space for learning. A story-telling radio programme from my childhood used to start with the words, "Are you sitting comfortably? Then I'll begin." Physical comfort is important. We will think about other forms of comfort later in the chapter. I don't know whether it is deliberate or accidental, but seats, chairs and pews in church premises always seem to feel uncomfortable – a reminder, perhaps, that you are not sitting there to enjoy yourself.

Physical discomfort is a distraction from learning. Part of the preparation for any learning event must be to ensure that the participants will be as comfortable as possible and that they can exercise personal preferences for using a chair or a cushion for sitting on the floor. Aspects such as the temperature of the room and the availability of drinking water are not trivial incidentals but essential to creating a physical environment conducive to learning.

Opening ourselves

I also have a concern about tables and desks. If you have papers or you want to make notes, a flat surface in front of you is very useful. It also puts a barrier between you and other people. I participate in many occasions where the seating is in the round but where we are sitting behind desks. The argument for this is always the utilitarian one. A few times the tables have been removed. Initially people feel uncomfortable. This is partly because it is not so easy to take notes, although in truth it is not that difficult. I suspect it is mainly because we feel more exposed to the others in the room without the barrier in front of us. It is easier for others to read us when we are all in view. We may fear that we have to be open to them. We may feel more protected and in control behind a barrier.

We cannot learn in a way that changes us without becoming vulnerable. It is easier to move the physical barriers behind which we can hide than the psychological protection with which we surround ourselves. We only develop trust within a group by proving ourselves to be trustworthy. Removing the physical protection is more that just shifting furniture; it is a powerful symbol of opening ourselves to one another.

Removing the physical barriers may change the way in which we work as a group. At the first meeting of the WCC's Commission on Education and Ecumenical Formation in 2001 we set the room up in the round without tables. Being a newly formed commission, it had no history to determine its style of meeting. However, other commissions in the past had operated on the style of business meetings and this may have been the expectation. We wanted this commission not so much to take documented decisions as to reflect on the nature and methodologies of education and ecumenical formation in the WCC. We did not want members to begin by discussing the content of papers on the table but rather to draw on their own experience and knowledge. My feeling after the five days together was that we would not have had such a rich discussion seated behind tables.

Appropriate arrangement

In thinking about this for the work of ecumenical education, we should recognize that there are no uniquely correct ways to arrange the seats. As in so many aspects, it is a matter of context and realism. To take the latter first, we can only do what is possible. Rows of seats screwed firmly to the floor cannot be moved momentarily. There always will be limitations. However, even in the most fixed or limited physical situation we can with imagination get people to interact despite the reality.

The context is more important. Assuming that we have chosen methodologies appropriate to the learning we are engaged in, there will be better ways of arranging the chairs. If a video is to be shown, it would be foolish to sit in a circle around the television monitor. There is nothing at all interesting about the back of a TV monitor. If the focus of interest is a screen, all participants need to have an uninterrupted view. In this case a horseshoe arrangement of seating may enable everyone to see the screen and one another. Another thing we often forget is that we can rearrange the seats appropriately for each learning activity. Our learning place does not have to remain in the same configuration throughout our time together.

Virtual space

All the reflection so far on the creation of space for learning has been on the basis of a physical space where people can interact. The understanding of community when we have thought about learning in community and being a learning community has been based on people already being in some kind of physical proximity or bringing them into that proximity. We also have to recognize the potential for ecumenical education of virtual space – that location of encounter and learning that can be created electronically.

Conversations with a group of young people working on an ecumenical project for online leadership development alerted me to an immense amount of description and reflection that exists on the challenges, strengths and weaknesses of creating virtual communities. On the whole this has not originated in the churches or the ecumenical movement. In Chapter 6, I mentioned the Internet as a means of providing information and how we could equip ourselves to learn with it. I pointed out that many academics saw the development of the Internet as being comparable to the invention of printing in its significance for humanity.

As we have seen with the ability to print books, technologies both reflect and shape cultures. They can alter our perceptions, redefine our values and even change the shape of our lives. It is not easy to predict in what ways this will happen. We must expect, though, that if the Internet is such a radical development, it will have a profound effect. The possibilities of creating virtual space in which virtual learning communities can grow may be as deeply disturbing to some as it is exciting to others.

It may help us think about virtual communities by looking at some of the characteristics of physical communities. Most of us relate to more than one community at once. Some of those may be geographical communities, for example, where we live, where we grew up or the work-place. However, some may not be based on living side by side in the same location but on other things that make us want to relate to others. We may belong to the community of those who learn together, follow the same profession, play in an orchestra together, belong to a political party, share environmental concerns or follow the same football team. Christian faith gives us a set of communities ranging from the local congregation to the world church. We are already familiar with a variety of physical communities that are about shared interests, either because we live together or because we choose to associate with each other.

Groups with shared interests proliferate on the Internet. You can find people coming together to interact around every topic under the sun. Online discussions that take place may be trivial or even indecent. This gives the Internet a bad reputation. At the other extreme, discussion may be very worthy and scholarly. Some discussions take place within a limited circle of committed members, others with a shifting membership. Groups may continue over a considerable period of time or may just be for the moment. Some virtual communities form because a group of people who have interacted with one another in a traditional setting want to continue their relationship and discussion. Others form because they attract like-minded people to join in. In either case, these are voluntary associations of people. Obviously, those who come together on the basis of existing relationships begin with an advantage. We do not yet know whether those who only meet through the Internet can make up the disadvantage over time.

The Internet has been described as an electronic agora, the market-place where the citizens of Athens met for conversation and political discussion, exchanging and testing ideas. The Internet may enable us to interact with people to whom we had no access before. The danger of any self-selected community, as a virtual community may be, is that there is no contradiction of difference to encourage the development of thinking or opening up of attitudes. This is also a kind of community from which some are excluded, although we should not be complacent about the accessibility of all to traditional physical community. People may be excluded from the conversation because they are not able to access the Internet. Although there is in general a North-South resource divide, there are exceptions both ways. There is also a psychological divide in the degree to which people are comfortable with the technology. We can describe this in terms of age, with younger people being more comfortable. However, my father in his nineties has recently acquired a computer and learned how to send e-mails and to access the Internet. The divide also probably has to do with conventional thinking, which could explain why church leaders often find this difficult.

At the moment there are significant difficulties in interacting in virtual space. Whether in the end these are inherent difficulties, only time and experience will tell. We have to remember that much of what we know about effective interaction in face-to-face groups has only been coherently articulated comparatively recently. Direct interpersonal conversation has several levels of communication – the words, how the words are said, the body language and the context in which the conversation takes place. In virtual space we can read the words and we may be able to ascertain the context, but the other two subtle but powerful elements are missing. Internet users have developed symbolic conventions to convey emotions. Once mastered these may help. However, they are intentional signs whereas in direct conversation we can often read much from the unintentional signs of body language. Unless you are an accomplished actor, it is difficult to be anyone else but yourself in face-to-face discourses. On the Internet you may mislead or deliberately confuse others by pretending to be what you are not. Another problem is that the conversation is permanently recorded. Literalists might welcome a word-for-word record, but most of us neither choose our words that carefully in conversation nor wish to be held to what we said earlier in a developing discourse.

On the positive side of virtual space, not being able to see or hear people removes some possibilities of prejudice. We are not able to jump to instantaneous judgments based on what they look or sound like. We can only judge by what they say. Also, for those participating there is equality of access to the conversation in a way that the exercise of power among group members often prevents.

We have at our disposal some well tried approaches to moderating groups. We know how to enable participation, to move discussion on, to assist group members to identify what they have done and what needs to be done, to respond to different moods and emotions in individuals and the whole group, to respect one another and so on. We know about the stages that groups go through in their development. What we do not yet know so well is how we do this kind of moderation in a virtual group.

We may need to create a variety of spaces, both physical and virtual, to support the many different kinds of human interactions and styles of community participation necessary for ecumenical education.

Safe space

This brings us to a totally different kind of rearrangement that is necessary to create space for learning. We might describe this as emotional or psychological space. We might describe it as spiritual space. In recent years there has been much talk of ecumenical space. In writing this I do not want to be tied down to anyone else's definition in these realms, yet I am indebted to them all.

A space for learning must be a safe space. It is a space where I can be myself without threat, psychological or physical. I need not be fearful of speaking of my experience, telling what I know and believe or sharing my hopes and dreams. I will be accepted as a person. My openness will not be abused. I will have to extend the same to all the other members of the group, even if I happen not to like them or what they say.

It is not a space where anything goes, where each one of us accepts uncritically what another has said or done. However, it is a space where we listen and think before we react, where questions are raised and counter opinions put without resorting to personal attack.

Although it is a safe space, it is also a disturbing space. A space where we all heard what we wanted to hear, where all our experience pointed in the same direction and where all agreed with every belief shared would not be a space of learning. It would either affirm existing knowledge or, more probably, reinforce our prejudices. Learning is often a painful business and creating a comfortable space will not serve us well.

This kind of open safety does not happen overnight, nor can it just be the result of skilful work by a facilitator. The level of trust can only be built up by the experience of the group. A group of people has to learn together how to create space so that further learning can happen.

A group of people drawn from different congregations had been meeting regularly as a part of an ecumenical course in Lent. One participant described how difficult he found it as a gay man in the congregation of which he was a part. This came as a surprise to the members of the group. Because the group had worked hard to develop a good level of trust among themselves, he had felt able to talk openly. The others had been able to listen, even though for some this was a very difficult thing to hear. In other contexts they might well have wanted to respond very negatively. Confronted by their own experience of him, however, they had to examine their own presuppositions.

One reason for creating this kind of learning space is to be able to interact openly. Another is to be able to play. For children, the safety of play spaces is usually described in terms of keeping dangers out and making sure that the internal environment has no damaging objects. Children's minds do not have to be set free in order to play. For adults the situation is reversed.

For children, play is one of the means by which they are able to try out life in safety. In play there are no long-lasting consequences of decisions or actions. Next time you can always be different or try something different. Play in childhood is not an idle diversion to pass the time happily until you are old enough to do real things. It is part of the way we prepare for the future. Adults need to play for similar reasons. In play we can try out various ways of thinking, acting and being without the usual consequences. As adults, though, we need the space to be created in which we can do this. We may think it beneath our dignity to pretend to be other than we are. We need protection from being critically observed. It is only in a safe space that we can fully enter into the role-play or the simulation.

Role-plays and simulations are often used in education relating to work where good personal interactions are important. I once attended a weekend residential management course where we were given role-plays around certain personnel problems. I do not know what the course tutor thought but I did not judge the exercise a great success. The outgoing characters threw themselves into their roles with great enthusiasm. Those more reserved in nature mumbled their way through. We played our parts but learned little from the experience. The right space had not been opened up for us to be able to seriously and sensitively explore in our roles how to deal with the situation presented. In our reflection on the experience we were only able to talk about what someone might have felt like or done in that situation. We ought to have been able to say how we felt and why we acted the way we did as the characters. I hope you can see the difference between the two outcomes. We could have achieved the first simply by reading the given scenario and discussing it. You can only produce the latter if the right space is created.

The ethos of a space can facilitate learning. One way in which this can be created is by the use of a visual focus, particularly in the centre of a circle. In a workshop on women's ways of learning, the participants were each asked to bring with them an object that was significant in their personal story. At the start of the workshop the participants placed their objects in the centre of the circle one by one and each told the story of its significance. That display and the experiences represented in it remained at the heart of the workshop for the remaining days. Sometimes a visual focus does not have to be so explicit. It could just be colour and patterns in flowers, cloths and other things to stimulate the senses.

In this chapter I have indicated the importance of creating an appropriate space in which ecumenical education may take place. It is about physical and psychological arrangements that have to be made with care. The creation of the right space does not guarantee good learning but is the fertile ground in which it may take place.

Conclusion
Moving On

Think back to Chapter 1, where you were asked to give your own meaning of the phrase "ecumenical education".

Now that you have reached the end of this book, how would you define ecumenical education in terms of its purpose and how it can be done?

In the introduction I asked whether ecumenical education should help us become map-readers or map-makers. I am convinced that the latter should be our aim. Learning to become a map-reader presumes that maps exist, that is, that we know how the world is and how it works. September 11, the day of the attacks on New York and Washington, has been identified by many as a day on which the world irrevocably changed. Only a longer perspective will tell whether it was another page of human history or the start of a new chapter. What we can already say is that the events of that day showed us how inaccurate our understanding of the world was. It also revealed the inadequacy of responses based on out-of-date maps. If we want a new world order where peace comes through just and mutual relationships, we need to be map-makers so that we may all move on.

Of course, map-readers versus map-makers is a false antithesis. You cannot be a map-maker without being a map-reader. However, you can be a map-reader without being a map-maker. One is so much more creative than the other is. Our human tragedy in so many things, including our faith, is that we settle for second best. We prefer to stay with what we already know and do instead of using all that to create the new. Yet we believe that as humans we are made in the image of God. Creativity should run through all that we are and all that we do.

This books gives no authoritative statement on what ecumenical education is or could be, no definitive learning objectives setting out what an ecumenically committed person or community should know and no model ecumenical curriculum. If I had given you these things, I would have been giving you a map and telling you how to read it!

A book is an imperfect medium for the kind of interaction we need to have to think about ecumenical education. By offering questions for consideration throughout the book, I have tried to engage you in the process. I would prefer to relate to you directly. At the end of this chapter you will find my e-mail address and an invitation to take our reflection on ecumenical education further.

Ecumenical education takes on as many different forms as there are contexts and needs. It will not be the same in a seminary in Asia, in a council of churches in Africa, in a social movement in Latin America or in an interdenominational group of individuals in Europe. That does not mean that we cannot identify common elements in terms of values and principles that permeate all ecumenical education.

There is a mind game that we religious people often play in relation to those of different traditions and other faiths. We take the great ideals of our own faith and compare them with the less than ideal actual practices of the other. In doing so, we conveniently ignore the great ideals of the other traditions and faiths and the way we subvert our faith's ideals in practice. We either lack self-knowledge or fail to exercise it. I say this because I see the values of ecumenical education as being based in Christ – the transformation of the life of individuals and communities into the life of the kingdom of God. In other words, the emphasis should be the ideals rather than the self-interested interpretation and practice of, for example, justice, forgiveness, peace, joy, openness, relationship and faith. Ecumenical education should explore both the meaning and the practice of such things. This is where ecumenical education serves the renewal of the church.

We do not have to make people learn. Learning is a natural process for human beings; we do it all the time. Our problems with learning come because we fail to recognize when this happens. As a consequence, we try to impose educational practices that ignore this and its outcomes. We try to work against the natural flow and processes. I have suggested some ways in which we can take seriously what we already know and adopt sympathetic methodologies. We need to take advantage of the immense amount we now know about our capacity for learning, our multi-faceted abilities and the mechanisms of learning.

We also need to recognize that learning is of the essence of Christian faith and, therefore, the ecumenical movement. We know truth and make meaning in dialogue. That may sometimes be a painful process – remember Jacob wrestling overnight with an unknown assailant at Peniel and learning his new name of Israel (Gen. 32:22–32) or Jesus in Gethsemane agonizing over God's purpose for him (Matt. 26:36–46). It is a much harder process than buying pre-packed propositions off the shelf. Yet justice will remain an empty concept until we learn how to act justly and so on. Educators often talk of the need to encourage lifelong learning. Discipleship is exactly that because, as Paul reminds us, in this life there is always more to know.

Encounter with the "other"

There is a management technique called a SWOT analysis – strengths, weaknesses, opportunities, threats. It can be a matter of interesting discussion whether something is an opportunity or a threat. All too often, we have seen those who are different from us in their belief, thought, behaviour or even appearance as a threat. We must engage with people from different traditions within the Christian faith and with those of other faiths because it helps us to develop better communal relations. Such engagements also help us with our own personal and spiritual development. Our personal and faith identities should be created alongside others' identities rather in opposition to them.

Interfaith or inter-religious learning is a necessity rather than an optional extra in a pluralistic world. Ecumenical education sees encounter with the other as an opportunity giving potential for personal and communal change. It makes use of those encounters that happen anyway and seeks to create even more. Encounter is not simply an opportunity to learn *from* others but *with* others. It is an opportunity to develop just relationships, to exercise acceptance and forgiveness.

As I have stressed, encounters on their own do not necessarily result in learning. Something has to happen with any experience to help us learn. We have labelled it reflection. It is about processing and understanding our experience in order not only to add to what we know but also to change our attitudes and behaviour. It is something we can do on our own but is best done in the company of others to bring a wider critique. There is always a danger that what we learn is self-serving.

We should never be content with forms of education that only reinforce the status quo, whether in the church or in society. However holy the church, however benign the society, neither are the kingdom of God. Change is not only desirable, it is necessary. Creative ecumenical education must nurture critical thinking. This enables us to see and act. Critical thinking is often felt to be a threat by the institutional church and the institutions of society. The nature of human institutions is that they are inherently conservative, with an instinct for self-preservation. Christians sometimes call critical thinking discernment. In doing so they may limit it to the spiritual and blunt its practical cutting edge.

The creation of what is called ecumenical space has been one of the more recent concerns of the ecumenical movement. This is space where all may enter freely and be able to interact safely with those whose differences might otherwise be threatening. This is the kind of space within which ecumenical learning can happen. The creation of such space, whether physical, psychological or virtual, requires careful consideration and planning. I have suggested that this is as significant for ecumenical education as the preparation of learning programmes. Without the right space, the kind of learning we desire will not happen or will be diminished.

Creative ecumenical education requires actual participation. It cannot be done second hand or by proxy. This means that we should not only engage people's minds but the whole of them. This has implications for our educational methods.

We cannot do the work of ecumenical education by sitting people down and instructing them. There are many learning activities we can use. To leave it there, however, would be to keep ecumenical education as a separated activity. Ecumenical education must be rooted in life. It should engage with people's lives and that is much more than involving body, mind and spirit in learning activities. Life as experienced and lived is the raw material of ecumenical education.

Much of what has been done in ecumenical education has focused on youth (actually young adults) and adults. All that I have written so far about individual learning has made no assumptions about the age of those individuals. For the past 30 years I have worked ecumenically to prepare learning material for all ages for use in congregations and churches. Children, young people and adults need to be engaged in ecumenical education in Sunday schools and other learning opportunities even in their denominational settings. I have been an advocate of intergenerational learning as opposed to age-divided learning. Ecumenical learning should include adults learning from children as well as children learning from adults. The challenge that remains is to change the mindset of congregations and for churches to adopt creative practices.

Educational processes have to be appropriate to the learners. This means that we have to be sensitive to their needs and capabilities. Simplistic stereotyping – for example, by age, gender or social class – often blinds us to the realities. To give one example of a traditional understanding of intelligence, a bright ten-year-old may be more intelligent than many adults in their community. Concepts of multiple intelligences should free us to see and value everyone. People usually have a greater capacity to learn than we credit. Our simplistic equation of the "academic" with quality needs to be rethought. This will benefit us in being able to value ecumenical education that follows other paths and the academic world where it needs reformation.

Ecumenical education has to take seriously the need for consistency between form and content. We cannot develop critical thinking using methods that require an uncritical acceptance. We cannot reflect on the implications of acting justly using methods that exploit or manipulate learners. This pushes us to explore the alternatives to schooling methodologies.

One of the constant themes of this book has been that ecumenical education is as much about the community as the individual. To most of us these days, the word education carries the implication of individual learning. When community is brought in it is either as the context of an individual's learning or with the hope that, by learning, the individual will improve the life of the community. This understanding ignores the need and the opportunity for communities to learn as communities. Ecumenical education is as much about local communities, congregations, churches and movements learning as it is about their individual members learning.

Another common presumption about education is that it is essentially concerned with handing on knowledge, concepts, skills, beliefs and so on. This view of education as transmission is shared by many in the churches and in the ecumenical movement. I do not want to deny the importance of handing on what we already know. The arguments for this are so prevalent that I need not repeat them. However, merely handing on knowledge fails to recognize two important dimensions. The first is that for transmitted knowledge to become meaningful to the learner it has to be owned by them as their knowledge and practised by them as their action. The second is that we cannot be content with what we already know and do. God always calls us into the new—the new relationship, the new community. Our skills, attitudes and knowledge need to be changed. To be true to the gospel, ecumenical education must be directed towards transformation. Change is not an option but a necessity.

But the aim is not any transformation nor the creation of any community. In ecumenical education our values are shaped by those of Jesus and embodied in his expression of the kingdom of God. We recognize our interconnectedness with creation, God and one another. This requires us to be open to others and to all that is around us and to use the skill of discernment. For us, justice is not an abstract concept or ideal. It is active, something to be done. We should be guided by the saying of St. Augustine, "Love and do what you will". Love does not mean that anything goes but demands the highest in terms of knowledge, relationships and actions.

Map making is about taking us from what is to what can be. In ecumenical education we take what is given to us in all its diversity. We take our contexts, ourselves and our faith traditions and learn together in order to create the new. It is an exercise of creativity and therefore of God.

> How can you create new ways of learning together in your context?
>
> What needs to be changed in your current educational activities so that they can become creative ecumenical education?

An invitation

I would like to think that after reading this book you will want to comment on my understanding of ecumenical education. Whether you agree or disagree with what I have written, you may want to offer alternative theories or your own experience and practice. Think of this as an opportunity, if you like, to learn more together.

Please e-mail me at
simon.oxley@wcc-coe.org
or write to me at

Education and Ecumenical Formation
World Council of Churches
150 route de Ferney
PO Box 2100
1211 Geneva 2
Switzerland

Suggestions for Further Reading

Where the content or relevance of the book is not self-evident from the title, I have added a brief note.

The ecumenical movement

G. Goosen, *Bringing Churches Together: A Popular Introduction to Ecumenism,* Geneva, WCC Publications, 2001.

M. Kinnamon & B.E. Cope, eds., *The Ecumenical Movement: An Anthology of Key Texts and Voices,* Geneva, WCC Publications, 1998.

M. VanElderen & M. Conway, *Introducing the World Council of Churches,* Geneva, WCC Publications, 2001.

Ecumenical education and learning

E. Appiah & G. Rüppell eds, *Empowering Lay Leadership: A Manual on Ecumenical Learning for Courses in Lay Leadership Training,* Geneva, WCC Education and Ecumenical Formation, 2000.

L. Bauerchose, *Learning to Live Together: Interchurch Partnerships as Ecumenical Communities of Learning,* Geneva, WCC Publications, 2001.

H.-R. Weber, *A Laboratory for Ecumenical Life: The Story of Bossey 1946–1996,* Geneva, WCC Publications, 1996. This account of the Ecumenical Institute, Bossey, contains many insights about the nature of ecumenical learning.

Education and learning in the Christian community

J.M. Hull, *What Prevents Christian Adults from Learning?,* London, SCM Press, 1985.

J. Sutcliffe, *Tuesday's Child: A Reader for Christian Educators,* Birmingham, Christian Education Publishing, 2001. Although basically focused on children, many of the extracts relate to all ages. It contains key passages from writers on the theology of education, the role of experience, the church community, participation in the liturgy and faith development theory.

L. Vogel, *Teaching and Learning in Communities of Faith: Empowering Adults through Religious Education,* San Francisco, Jossey-Bass, 1991.

Education and learning in general

T. Buzan, *The Mindmap Book,* London, BBC Books, 1995. This sets out ways of creative thinking using diagrammatic representations.

P. Freire, *Pedagogy of Freedom,* Lanham MD, Rowman & Littlefield, 2001.

P. Freire, *Pedagogy of the Oppressed,* New York, Seabury, 1970.

H. Gardner, *Intelligence Reframed: Multiple Intelligences for the 21st Century,* New York, Basic Books, 1999. This includes a review of his earlier writing on multiple intelligences, consideration of new categories and guidance on the use of the theory in education.

S.B. Merriam & R.S. Caffarella, *Learning in Adulthood: A Comprehensive Guide,* San Francisco, Jossey-Bass, 1999. A thorough overview of adult development, the learning process and the practice of adult education.

P.M. Senge, *The Fifth Discipline: The Art and Practice of the Learning Organization,* New York, Doubleday, 1994. Although this is oriented towards commercial organizations, it contains much of value for individual and collective learning in voluntary associations and faith communities.